文部科学省後援 技術英検

技術英語
ハンドブック

JSTC 公益社団法人 日本工業英語協会
JAPAN SOCIETY FOR TECHNICAL COMMUNICATION

技術英検2・3級用
【基礎例文500】
【基礎単語1600】

JN063274

日本能率協会マネジメントセンター

工業英検から技術英検へ

〈試験概要〉

受験資格
受験資格は一切ありません。どなたでも受験できます。

試験日
年 3 回実施（プロフェッショナルは年 2 回のみ実施）
＊詳細は下記ホームページをご確認ください。

試験形式

各級	出題形式	対象	団体受験
プロフェッショナル	記述式	科学・技術分野の英語文書を読みこなし、かつ正しく、明確に、簡潔に書くことができる。文書のスタイルは種類（マニュアル,仕様書,論文等）に応じて異なることを理解しており、正しく使いわけることができる。	×
準プロフェッショナル			
1 級	選択式／記述式	科学・技術に関する英文を読むことができる。英文資料の要約、議事録、英文 E-mail 等の短文が書ける。	○
2 級	選択式	科学・技術英語の語彙力があり、構文・文法を理解している。	○
3 級	選択式	科学・技術英語の基礎的な語彙力があり、構文の基礎を理解している。	○

検定料（公開会場料金／税込）

プロフェッショナル	準プロフェッショナル	1 級	2 級	3 級
￥16,500		￥6,400	￥5,300	￥2,600

＊「プロフェッショナル」「準プロフェッショナル」は同一の問題となり、得点率に応じての判定となります。

一般社団法人日本能率協会 JSTC 技術英語委員会

〒 105-0011 東京都港区芝公園 3-1-22

● TEL：03-3434-2350　● E-mail：info@jstc.jp　● HP：https://jstc.jma.or.jp

<u>まえがき</u>

　企業の国際化を背景に、英語はますます重要なものとなってきました。特に、技術英語は技術の進歩とともに必須の知識として認識され始めています。

　しかしながら、技術英語は一般英語と違って、参考書の種類・数も限られており、勉強のすすめ方などで困っている人も多いのが現状です。

　このような状況を背景に、小会では、一般英語から技術英語への橋渡しとしての英語教材をハンドブックの形で刊行することとなりました。

　ここに収録した例文・単語は、現場から集めたものと技術英語検定試験に出題されたものの中から基礎的なものを選んでありますので、初めて学ばれる方から、ある程度の知識を持った方のための復習・整理用としても利用できます。

　技術英語は技術者・研究者のみならず、国際的に活躍するビジネスマンにとっても、その基礎的な知識は、不可欠なものとなっています。

　ぜひ、本書をご一読いただき、日頃の学習にご活用くだされば幸いです。例文の収集・チェックにあたり、小会の技術英検推進委員の方々にご尽力をいただきました。ここに深く感謝の意を表します。

本書の特色と使い方

☆ 携帯に便利な**ポケットサイズ**のため、通勤・通学時での学習用として大変便利です。

☆ 例文編・単語編に分かれており、**例文編**では、現場で常用される計 500 の表現を、やさしいものから順に英文対訳形式で載せています。**単語編**では、専門にとらわれない技術英語の基礎的な単語をアルファベット順に計 1,600 語網羅しています。

☆ 一般の方々だけでなく、工業高校・工業高等専門学校・大学の理工学部の学生などが、一般英語から**技術英語**へと学び始める際の**補助テキスト**として利用することができます。

☆ 初めて技術英語を学ばれる方は、英文を中心に**技術英語の特徴**を、またある程度技術英語を学ばれた方は、和文を中心に**適切な英文表現**を勉強してください。

☆ 例文編の後半では技術英検の 2・3 級の英文和訳、和文英訳の問題として過去に出題されたものを載せてありますので、**技術英検の受験対策用**としても役立てられます。

☆ 同様の例文が重複している場合がありますが、重要なものですので**繰り返し学習**してください。

☆ 例文・単語の使用頻度に応じて、例文の番号欄、単語の□欄に**チェック**や**色分け**などを施すことによって、繰り返し学習する際の指針とすることができます。

基礎例文 *500*

1.　The alarm is ringing.

2.　The light will not go on.

3.　Remove the oil stain.

4.　Alcohol dissolves resins.

5.　The switches are all off.

6.　The manual is difficult to understand.

7.　The conveyor is being repaired.

8.　Draw a diagonal line.

9.　A floppy disk is lying on the floor.

10.　The iron bar is deteriorating.

11.　Turn the box upside down.

12.　This spring is very durable.

13.　The cable snapped.

14.　Put the piece on the workbench.

15.　This material is too brittle.

16.　The fuel tank is empty.

17.　We are five welding rods short.

18.　There were as many as ten victims.

19.　Drill a hole in this panel.

20.　Those gloves are hard to put on.

1.　警報が鳴っている。

2.　ライトがつかない。

3.　油の汚れを取りなさい。

4.　アルコールは樹脂を溶解する。

5.　スイッチはすべて切れている。

6.　そのマニュアルは分かりにくい。

7.　コンベアは補修中です。

8.　対角線を引きなさい。

9.　フロッピーディスクが床に落ちている。

10.　その鉄棒は腐食している。

11.　箱をひっくり返しなさい。

12.　このバネはとても耐久性がある。

13.　ケーブルが切れた。

14.　その部品を作業台に乗せなさい。

15.　この材料はもろすぎる。

16.　燃料タンクが空である。

17.　溶接棒が5本足りない。

18.　被害者が10人もいた。

19.　このパネルに穴をあけなさい。

20.　その手袋ははめにくい。

21. Everything went smoothly.

22. Do not forget to do periodic maintenance.

23. Paint was spilt on the floor.

24. The tip of the soldering iron was missing.

25. The knife's blade is chipped.

26. Explain it in more detail.

27. Arrange these boxes lengthwise.

28. Two bolts were found broken.

29. Maximum speed was reached.

30 The capacity includes tolerance.

31. This wire has low resistance.

32. This old model is not recommended.

33. Oil was leaking from the pipes.

34. This valve is defective.

35. The cutting tool cuts well.

36. Peel off the tape carefully.

37. The project was completed as scheduled.

38. The quality has deteriorated.

39. Turn down the burner flame.

21.　すべてが順調に進んだ。

22.　定期点検を忘れずに行うこと。

23.　塗料が床にこぼれていた。

24.　はんだこての先がなかった。

25.　ナイフの刃が欠けている。

26.　もっと詳しく説明してください。

27.　これらの箱を縦に並べなさい。

28.　ボルトが２本折れていることが分かった。

29.　最高速度に達した。

30　容量にゆとりがある。

31.　このワイヤは抵抗値が低い。

32.　この古いモデルはお勧めできない。

33.　配管から油が漏れていた。

34.　このバルブには欠陥がある。

35.　このバイトはよく切れる。

36.　テープは丁寧にはがしなさい。

37.　そのプロジェクトは計画どおりに完成した。

38.　品質が低下した。

39.　バーナーの炎を小さくしなさい。

40. This engine requires a tune-up.

41. Keep the set horizontal.

42. Load the camera with film.

43. Computer control is not always safe.

44. Something is wrong with the machine.

45. Finish that by tomorrow.

46. The computer doesn't work.

47. This machine weighs about 30 kg.

48. Too much load causes overheating.

49. A film of oil was floating on the water.

50. There are two types of telescopes.

51. Take up the slack in the tape.

52. There is a skid mark on the workshop floor.

53. Cracks and deformations were found.

54. The equipment is ready for operation.

55. No one has submitted a report yet.

56. The transit instrument is slanted a little.

57. Explain the structure of the microwave oven.

40.　このエンジンは調整が必要である。

41.　装置を水平にしておきなさい。

42.　カメラにフィルムを装填しなさい。

43.　コンピュータ制御がいつも安全だとは限らない。

44.　機械の調子が変だ。

45.　明日までにそれを終えなさい。

46.　コンピュータが作動しない。

47.　この機械の重さは30kgぐらいある。

48.　荷重の掛けすぎがオーバーヒートの原因だ。

49.　水面には油の膜が浮いていた。

50.　望遠鏡には２つの型式がある。

51.　テープのたるみを取り除きなさい。

52.　工場の床にスリップした跡がある。

53.　亀裂や歪みが生じていた。

54.　その装置は作動する状態になっている。

55.　まだ誰も報告書を提出していない。

56.　トランシットが少し傾いている。

57.　電子レンジの構造を説明しなさい。

58. The results of the pressure test were not good.

59. The drawings conflicted with the specifications.

60. The whole structure started trembling.

61. Have the engine already running.

62. Place A parallel to B.

63. The brake drum was worn.

64. The lens is out of focus.

65. The pantograph often emits sparks.

66. That material changes shape when heated.

67. Halley's Comet can be seen every 76 years.

68. Tighten the screw with a screwdriver.

69. Have him check the steam pressure.

70. Turning the knob to the left turns on the water.

71. Always wear goggles when welding.

72. It was decided to order the computer from Company A.

73. The experiment will succeed if this procedure is followed.

58.　圧力試験の成績は不良であった。

59.　図面と仕様書が食い違っていた。

60.　その構造物全体が揺れ始めた。

61.　エンジンをあらかじめかけておくこと。

62.　AとBを平行に置きなさい。

63.　ブレーキドラムがすり減っていた。

64.　レンズのピントがずれている。

65.　パンタグラフから火花がよく出る。

66.　その材料は熱を加えると変形する。

67.　ハレー彗星は76年ごとに見られる。

68.　ねじをねじ回し（ドライバ）で締めなさい。

69.　蒸気の圧力を彼に調べさせなさい。

70.　そのつまみを左に回すと水が出る。

71.　溶接する時は、必ず眼鏡をかけなさい。

72.　A社にそのコンピュータを注文することに
　　なった。

73.　実験はこの手続きに従えば成功する。

74. Watch the waveform on the CRT carefully.

75. It will take ten days to finish that work.

76. The bolt cannot be removed no matter what tool is used.

77. Have the engineer, Mr. Tanaka make the bird's-eye-view drawing.

78. If water and oil are mixed, they will emulsify.

79. This machine was imported from the U.S.

80. Turning the switch will ring the bell.

81. Draw the plan on a scale of 1 to 100.

82. According to the report, the work was cancelled.

83. The pliers are next to the tool boxes.

84. If the wrong tool is chosen, the job will not be completed successfully.

85. A 100 HP motor will be used.

86. Do not raise the pressure in the tank any higher.

87. Plastics can be plated.

88. Pull the lever toward you.

74.　ＣＲＴ上の波形をよく監視しなさい。

75.　その仕事を終えるには10日かかるだろう。

76.　何を用いても、そのボルトは外れない。

77.　鳥瞰図は田中技師に描いてもらいなさい。

78.　水と油を一緒に混ぜると乳状になる。

79.　この機械はアメリカから輸入された。

80.　そのスイッチをひねるとベルが鳴る。

81　平面図は１/100の縮尺で描きなさい。

82.　報告によると、その工事は中止になった。

83.　ペンチは道具箱の横にある。

84.　工具の選択を誤ると作業はうまくいかない。

85.　モータは100馬力のものを使用する。

86.　タンク内の圧力をそれ以上、上げてはいけない。

87.　プラスチックにめっきすることができる。

88.　レバーを手前に引いてください。

89. The mechanical pencil has run out of lead.

90. Be careful when using that cutter.

91. The experiment was a failure because the air was polluted.

92. Complex procedures are necessary.

93. Tomorrow, the client will pay us four million yen.

94. The fuel is running short.

95. The world's largest refracting telescope is in the U.S.

96. Concrete consists of cement, sand, and gravel.

97. A Phillips screwdriver is needed to remove this screw.

98. Fill this beaker with water.

99. That condition is described on page 100 of the manual.

100. Pass the liquid through a strainer.

101. Solar energy does not pollute the air.

102. Two posts are broken.

103. Watch your step.

104. The screwdriver was completely rusted.

105. This material is hard to process.

89. シャープペンシルの芯がなくなっている。

90. そのカッターの取り扱いに注意しなさい。

91. 空気が汚れていたので実験は失敗だった。

92. 複雑な手続きが必要だ。

93. 明日、顧客から400万円の支払いがある。

94. 燃料が残り少なくなった。

95. 世界で最大の屈折式望遠鏡はアメリカにある。

96. コンクリートはセメント、砂、砂利でできている。

97. このねじを外すにはプラスのねじ回しが必要だ。

98. このビーカーに水をいっぱい入れなさい。

99. その条件はマニュアルの100ページに述べてある。

100. その液体を濾過器に通しなさい。

101. 太陽エネルギーは空気を汚染しない。

102. 柱が2本折れている。

103. 足元に注意しなさい。

104. ねじ回しがすっかりさびていた。

105. この材料は加工しにくい。

106. Proteins are widely used as foaming agents.

107. The material is fed from above.

108. The material is heated here.

109. He is used to operating this machine.

110. We reduced production by 10%.

111. Here, the material is carefully selected.

112. This rule takes effect from next month.

113. This rope was broken.

114. If the plating is inferior, the metal will easily rust.

115. Pick out a specimen from the lot.

116. Don't go near the machine.

117. The current must be switched off at the main power switch.

118. Touching the machine is dangerous.

119. The span is taking a very heavy strain.

120. The delayed delivery of parts upset the program.

121. Applying oil will make it slide smoothly.

106. たんぱく質は、発泡剤として広く利用されている。

107. 材料は上から供給される。

108. 素材はここで加熱される。

109. 彼はこの機械の操作に慣れている。

110. 生産量を10%減らした。

111. ここで材料が厳選される。

112. この規則は来月から有効である。

113. このロープが切れていた。

114. めっきが不良だと、金属はさびが出やすい。

115. ロットから見本を抜き出しなさい。

116. 機械に近寄らないでください。

117. 電流はメインスイッチで切らなければならない。

118. その機械に触れると危険だ。

119. スパンに非常に大きなひずみがかかっている。

120. 部品の納入が遅れて計画が狂った。

121. 油を塗れば滑りが良くなる。

122. We call the lathe the "king of machines."

123. Do it the same way as last time.

124. Company A was slow in dealing with the matter.

125. Total and tabulate the measured values.

126. Do not leave combustible materials around here.

127. This machine tool is made in Sweden.

128. We can't recommend this method to anyone.

129. Water is spouting from the hose.

130. Bend this into three parts.

131. The spindles have already been replaced.

132. Pulling the cord is dangerous.

133. Exchange the right and left components.

134. The steel is left to cool until it becomes dark-red.

135. This model is built on a scale of one to ten.

136. Omitting periodic maintenance will result in repair problems.

137. The error is within the allowable limits.

122.　われわれは、旋盤を「機械の王」と呼んでいる。

123.　前回と同じ方法で行いなさい。

124.　A社はその件について対応が遅れた。

125.　測定結果を集計して表にしなさい。

126.　周囲に燃えやすい物を置いてはいけない。

127.　この工作機械はスウェーデン製である。

128.　この方法は誰にも勧められない。

129.　水がホースから噴き出している。

130.　これを３つに折りなさい。

131.　心棒の交換はすでに終わっている。

132.　コードを引っ張ると危険だ。

133.　左右の部品を入れ替えなさい。

134.　鋼は赤黒い色になるまで放置して冷やす。

135.　この模型は10分の１の縮尺である。

136.　保守を怠ると、後の修理が面倒になる。

137.　誤差は許容範囲である。

138. This product conforms to safety standards.

139. The material is heat-treated in this furnace.

140. The operation standards need to be reexamined.

141. Pieces of iron flew in all directions.

142. An hour's drive will take us to the plant.

143. Have this ready by tomorrow morning.

144. Pulling the string will ring the bell.

145. The direct cause of the breakdown is rust.

146. The temperature is ten degrees below zero Celsius.

147. Do you have any questions on this process?

148. The product is painted twice and baked.

149. Quenching and tempering are repeated several times.

150. How long does this process take?

151. This wire is one micron or less in diameter.

152. The ingot is heated until it becomes white-hot.

138.　この製品は安全基準に適合している。

139.　材料はこの炉の中で熱処理される。

140.　その作業標準は再検討が必要だ。

141.　鉄片が四方八方に飛び散った。

142.　工場までは、車で1時間かかるだろう。

143.　明朝までにこれを用意しなさい。

144.　その紐を引っ張るとベルが鳴る。

145.　故障の直接の原因はさびである。

146.　温度は零下10℃である。

147.　この工程について何か質問はありませんか。

148.　製品は2回塗装して、焼き付けられる。

149.　焼き入れと焼き戻しは数回繰り返される。

150.　この工程には、どのくらい時間がかかりますか。

151.　このワイヤの直径は1ミクロン以下である。

152.　インゴットは白熱するまで加熱される。

153. Fill the cup half full of water.

154. You have to mount the part in the prescribed position.

155. This furnace burns heavy oil for the heat treatment process.

156. The sound of a jet plane is an example of noise pollution.

157. The expansion and contraction of a tube produces stress.

158. The electrical system is faulty.

159. Turn the lid counterclockwise to remove it.

160. Don't look directly at the intense light.

161. The motor is always test run once.

162. This lathe was imported from Germany.

163. What are the chemical properties of ammonia?

164. Flipping this switch up turns on the light.

165. They strike the material with a hammer to judge the quality.

166. This furnace is 100 cubic meters large.

167. There is a slight vibration at around 120 mph.

153.　そのコップに水を半分入れなさい。

154.　部品を所定の位置に取り付けなさい。

155.　この炉は熱処理用に重油を炊く。

156.　ジェット機の音は騒音公害の一つである。

157.　管の伸縮によって応力が生じる。

158.　電気系統に異常がある。

159.　蓋（ふた）を外すには、左（反時計方向）に回しなさい。

160.　強い光を直接見ないようにしなさい。

161.　モータは必ず一度試運転しておく。

162.　この旋盤は、ドイツから輸入されたものである。

163.　アンモニアの化学特性は何ですか。

164.　このスイッチを上にすると明かりがつく。

165.　素材をハンマで叩いてその品質を判定する。

166.　この炉の大きさは100m³である。

167.　時速120マイルあたりで軽い振動がある。

168. Never throw water on an organic solvent fire.

169. Keep pressing it until the adhesive dries.

170. This factory consists of three major divisions.

171. Product finishing takes about one hour.

172. Clear the aisle and let the cart through.

173. Do not operate the machine if the red light is on.

174. Have him check the boiler pressure.

175. This product is exported in large quantities.

176. It is on the third line from the bottom of this page.

177. This machine is computer-controlled.

178. Prevent foreign matter from getting into the test tube.

179. The knob is out of position.

180. Why does it have to be processed quickly?

181. If the prime coat is imperfect, the finish coat will also be imperfect.

182. Investigation revealed some serious mistakes.

168. 有機溶剤の火災には水をかけてはならない。

169. 接着剤が乾くまで押さえていてください。

170. この工場は、大きく3つの部門に分かれている。

171. 製品の仕上げ工程にはおよそ1時間かかる。

172. 通路を空けて、カートを通してやりなさい。

173. 赤いライトが点灯している時は、その機械を動かしてはならない。

174. ボイラの圧力を彼に調べてもらいなさい。

175. この製品は大量に輸出されている。

176. それはこのページの下から3行目に書いてある。

177. この機械はコンピュータ制御されている。

178. 試験管へ異物が入らないようにしなさい。

179. つまみの位置がずれている。

180. なぜ、その処理を早くしなければならないのですか。

181. 下塗りが不良だと、仕上げ塗りも不良になる。

182. 調査によって重大な誤りが発見された。

183.　A current leaking from the cable was detected.

184.　Incorrect operation will damage the functions.

185.　An induction motor works on alternating current.

186.　The driving unit is a 100-horsepower engine.

187.　The vibration of this model is kept to a minimum.

188.　Keep it covered so that it does not spill.

189.　An iron hammer cannot be used because it causes dangerous sparks.

190.　Here, they have been researching steel heat treatment for 20 years.

191.　Choosing the wrong time for heat treatment can cause a reject.

192.　The rope should not be slackened, even a little.

193.　The spilt oil is spreading over the surface of the sea.

194.　This plant has an area of 10,000 square meters.

195.　If the engine does not work, the electrical system is probably out of order.

183.　そのケーブルから漏電<ruby>漏電<rt>ろうでん</rt></ruby>していることが分かった。

184.　操作が不正確だと機能が損なわれる。

185.　誘導電動機は交流で動く。

186.　駆動機には100馬力エンジンを用いている。

187.　この機種では振動を最小限に抑えてある。

188.　こぼれないように<ruby>蓋<rt>ふた</rt></ruby>をしておきなさい。

189.　危険な火花が発生するので鉄のハンマは使えない。

190.　ここでは鋼の熱処理の研究を20年間続けている。

191.　熱処理時間を誤ると不良品が発生する（オシャカになる）ことがある。

192.　そのロープは、少しでもたるませてはいけない。

193.　流出した油が海面に広がっている。

194.　この工場の面積は10,000㎡である。

195.　エンジンが作動しない場合は、たいてい電気系統の故障だ。

196. This place is very dangerous, so please pay attention to the signs.

197. If the cutting tool is chipped even a little, it will not cut satisfactorily.

198. The power was off for three hours yesterday.

199. Polishing has made this surface look like a mirror.

200. To do this work skillfully, more than ten years experience is required.

201. The radius is one half of the diameter.

202. This car has front disc brakes.

203. The quantity is so small that it cannot be detected.

204. This model is more fuel efficient than the previous ones.

205. Draw a circle with a compass.

206. Machines make work proceed faster.

207. Figure 2 shows the drive section.

208. Compare the totals.

209. The brake was quickly applied.

210. Gold is the best conductor.

211. A cube has six surfaces.

196.　ここは危険が多いので、標識には注意しなさい。

197.　バイトが少しでも欠けていたら、切削^{せっさく}はうまくできない。

198.　昨日は3時間停電した。

199.　この表面が鏡のように仕上がっているのは研磨による。

200.　この作業を上手に行うためには10年以上の経験が必要である。

201.　半径は直径の1/2である。

202.　この車は前輪がディスクブレーキである。

203.　あまりにも微量なので検出不可能だ。

204.　この機種は以前のものより燃費が良い。

205.　コンパスを使って円を描きなさい。

206.　機械を使うと仕事が早くできる。

207.　図2は駆動部を示している。

208.　総量を比較しなさい。

209.　すぐにブレーキがかけられた。

210.　金は伝導性が最もよい。

211.　立方体には面が6つある。

212. This method is economical.

213. Turn the knob clockwise.

214. Water is a stable compound.

215. Wheels with teeth are called gears.

216. Dampers control the gas flow.

217. Open the circuit breaker.

218. Acid rain is one of the biggest pollution problems.

219. Water freezes at zero degrees centigrade.

220. Carbon dioxide is composed of carbon and oxygen.

221. Things that contain iron stick to a magnet.

222. A lens is used to make things look larger or smaller.

223. A loudspeaker works very much like a telephone receiver.

224. This type of engine needs very little maintenance.

225. This factory has a product capacity of 12,000 tons daily.

226. Operate the machine after adjusting it.

212. この方法は経済的である。

213. つまみを右（時計方向）に回しなさい。

214. 水は安定した化合物である。

215. 歯のついているホイールが歯車である。

216. ダンパーはガスの流れを調整する。

217. 回路遮断機を切りなさい。

218. 酸性雨は重大な環境汚染問題の一つである。

219. 水は摂氏0度で凍る。

220. 二酸化炭素は炭素と酸素で構成されている。

221. 鉄を含む物は磁石にくっつく。

222. レンズは物を大きく見せたり、小さく見せたりするのに使われる。

223. 拡声器は、電話の受話器と同様の機能を持つ。

224. このタイプのエンジンは、ほとんど保守の必要はない。

225. この工場の生産能力は、日産12,000トンである。

226. 調整をしてから機械を動かしなさい。

227. This manual describes how to assemble the kit.

228. The contractor failed to complete the job on time.

229. Thorough treatment, not tentative measures, is needed.

230. Personal computers are difficult to learn to use.

231. The new machine is for removing snow.

232. An elastic material returns to its original shape.

233. This drill is 8.0 mm in diameter.

234. The reaction occurs in the absence of alcohol.

235. The needle of a compass indicates north and south.

236. Be sure to turn off the heater when leaving this room.

237. Adequate lubrication prevents the bearings from overheating.

238. This robot is constructed very ingeniously.

239. Water does not boil unless you heat it to 100℃.

240. Oxygen is carried through the body by blood.

227. このマニュアルにはキットの組み立て方が書いてある。

228. 業者はその仕事を納期内に仕上げなかった。

229. 応急処置ではなく、根本的な処置が必要だ。

230. パソコンの使用方法を学ぶことは難しい。

231. その新しい機械の目的は除雪である。

232. 弾力性のある物質はもとの形に戻る。

233. これは直径が8.0mmのドリルである。

234. この反応はアルコールがない状態で起こる。

235. コンパスの針は南北を指す。

236. この部屋を出るときは、必ずヒータのスイッチを切りなさい。

237. 注油を十分にすれば、ベアリングが過熱することはない。

238. このロボットは非常に精巧にできている。

239. 水は、温度を100℃まで上げないと沸騰しない。

240. 酸素は体内を血液によって運ばれる。

241. Heat has the property of changing a liquid into a gas.

242. Action and reaction are equal in magnitude and opposite in direction.

243. Regular maintenance extends the machine's life.

244. An electric heater is used for heating substances.

245. Not all parts of a magnet have equal attraction.

246. Good planning keeps production costs down.

247. A thick layer of paint will take a long time to dry.

248. A cloud is a mass of vapor in the sky.

249. Sound is produced by vibrating materials.

250. The extension cord is 2 meters long.

251. Clean the lens with alcohol.

252. Use rubber packings to prevent oil leaks.

253. Arrange the desks in two rows.

254. We conduct a non-destructive test to see if there is a defect.

255. The screw is loosened by vibration.

241.　熱は液体を気体に変える特性を持っている。

242.　作用と反作用は、大きさが等しいが、方向が反対である。

243.　定期保守は機械の寿命を延ばす。

244.　電熱器は物を熱するのに使われる。

245.　磁石は、どの部分も同じ吸引力があるとは限らない。

246.　計画が良ければ生産コストは下がる。

247.　厚く塗ったペンキは乾くのに時間がかかる。

248.　雲は空中の大量の蒸気の集まりである。

249.　音は物体の振動によって生じる。

250.　その延長コードの長さは2mである。

251.　レンズの表面をアルコールで拭きなさい。

252.　ゴムのパッキングを使って、オイル漏れを防ぎなさい。

253.　机を横に2列に並べなさい。

254.　非破壊検査で欠陥の有無を調べる。

255.　ねじは振動でゆるくなる。

256. Once taken apart, it is hard to put back together again.

257. Inspect the hoses and connections for leaks.

258. Mild steel contains up to 0.25% carbon.

259. Wear gloves for this operation.

260. The moment the switch was turned on, it sparked.

261. Machinery has been taking over work done by humans.

262. These two lines are at right angles to each other.

263. Show the dimensions in metric.

264. There are many types of damage to parts.

265. Heat caused that metal to melt.

266. Most mechanical equipment uses gears.

267. Pull the camshaft and release it.

268. Most cars use water to cool the engine.

269. The latest machinery was installed in the factory.

270. A large current flowing through a wire makes it hot.

256.　分解してしまうと、もとどおりにするのは難しい。

257.　ホースや接続に漏れがないか検査しなさい。

258.　軟鋼の炭素含有量は最大限0.25%である。

259.　この作業には手袋をはめなさい。

260.　スイッチを入れた瞬間、火花が出た。

261.　機械が、人間の仕事に取って代わってきている。

262.　この２本の直線は直角をなしている。

263.　寸法はメートル法で示しなさい。

264.　部品の損傷にはいろいろな種類がある。

265.　熱のためにその金属は融けた。

266.　ほとんどの機械装置には歯車が使ってある。

267.　カムシャフトを手前に引っ張って放しなさい。

268.　たいていの車はエンジンの冷却に水を使う。

269.　最新の機械類が工場に設置された。

270.　大電流が流れると電線は熱くなる。

271.　Oil in the bearings reduces friction.

272.　The method makes a great difference in the yield.

273.　He drove a nail into the wall.

274.　Adding 5 to 5 gives 10.

275.　A knife is a tool for cutting things.

276.　Space has no air; it is a vacuum.

277.　Defective parts can be replaced.

278.　A thermostat maintains the desired temperature.

279.　This transistor circuit appears to be in good condition.

280.　Oxygen is needed to burn things.

281.　The moon shines because it reflects the sun's light.

282.　Most brakes use friction to reduce speed.

283.　Bronze is an alloy of copper and tin.

284.　This computer is user-friendly and seldom breaks down.

285.　Plants grow well in rich soil.

286.　Water is a compound of hydrogen and oxygen.

271.　ベアリングの注油は摩擦を減らす。

272.　その方法だと歩留まりが大きく違ってくる。

273.　彼は壁に釘を打った。

274.　5足す5は10になる。

275.　ナイフは物を切る道具である。

276.　宇宙には空気がなく真空である。

277.　不良部品は取り替えることができる。

278.　サーモスタットは所定の温度を維持する。

279.　このトランジスタ回路は良い状態にあるようだ。

280.　物は燃えるとき、酸素を必要とする。

281.　月は太陽の光を反射して輝く。

282.　ほとんどのブレーキは摩擦を利用して減速する。

283.　青銅は銅と錫の合金である。

284.　このコンピュータは操作性が良く、ほとんど故障しない。

285.　植物は肥えた土地ではよく育つ。

286.　水は水素と酸素の化合物である。

287. This car has a maximum speed of 200 km per hour.

288. Like solids, most liquids expand when heated.

289. Some gases are heavier than air; others are lighter.

290. This solid will vaporize when heated.

291. Oxygen, hydrogen, and potassium are all elements.

292. Liquids take the shape of their container.

293. The average temperature of the area is 20℃.

294. A transformer raises or lowers the voltage.

295. High temperatures soften metals.

296. Warm air is lighter than cold air.

297. The earth is similar to an orange in shape.

298. Subtracting 3 from 8 leaves 5.

299. When ice is heated, it turns into a liquid.

300. Wood conducts sound better than air.

301. Heat the water until it boils away.

302. Ailerons help steer the airplane.

287.　この車の最高速度は時速200㎞である。

288.　固体と同じように、たいていの液体は加熱すると膨脹する。

289.　気体の中には空気よりも重いものもあり、軽いものもある。

290.　この固体は熱を加えると蒸気になる。

291.　酸素、水素、カリウムはすべて元素である。

292.　液体は容器に応じた形をとる。

293.　その地域の平均温度は摂氏20度である。

294.　変圧器は電圧を上げたり下げたりする。

295.　温度が高くなると金属はやわらかくなる。

296.　温かい空気は冷たい空気よりも軽い。

297.　地球はオレンジと似た形をしている。

298.　8から3を引くと5が残る。

299.　氷を熱すると液体に変わる。

300.　木材は空気よりも音をよく伝える。

301.　沸騰してなくなるまで水を熱しなさい。

302.　補助翼は飛行機の操縦に役立つ。

303.　Be careful not to mistake the reverse side for the front.

304.　Chemical elements are the basic constituents of all matter.

305.　Don't run hot water through this filter.

306.　This plastic bucket holds 10 liters.

307.　Pull the handle while pushing the red button on the board.

308.　The front panel has thirty-six switches.

309.　It will be all right if the error is one millimeter or less.

310.　This boiler is very popular because of its low fuel consumption.

311.　Stainless steel is an alloy that does not rust.

312.　A damaged cord could give the user an electric shock.

313.　Most substances are composed of two or more elements.

314.　A condenser is a device that converts vapor into liquid.

315.　The load divided by the cross-sectional area of the piston gives the pressure.

303.　表と裏を間違えないようにしなさい。

304.　化学元素はすべての物質の基本構成要素である。

305.　このフィルターに熱湯を流してはならない。

306.　このプラスチックバケツには10ℓ 入る。

307.　ボードの赤いボタンを押しながらハンドルを引きなさい。

308.　フロントパネルにはスイッチが36個ある。

309.　誤差は 1 ㎜以下であれば問題はない。

310.　このボイラーは燃料消費が少ないのでとても評判が良い。

311.　ステンレスはさびない合金である。

312.　痛んだコードはユーザを感電させる可能性がある。

313.　ほとんどの物質は 2 つ以上の元素でできている。

314.　コンデンサは、蒸気を液体に変える機械である。

315.　荷重をピストンの断面積で割ると、圧力が得られる。

316. This battery can be used for five consecutive hours.

317. To go to another planet, we must travel through space.

318. Alloys may have properties that pure metals do not.

319. In a chemical reaction, substance is neither gained nor lost.

320. Lubrication makes machinery run smoothly and quietly.

321. That company markets several new products every year.

322. To obtain a quarter of this number, we must divide it by four.

323. Gases are generally lighter than liquids and solids.

324. Ice loses some of its volume when it turns to water.

325. The ratio of 7 m to 1 m is written as 7:1 or 7/1.

326. Nitrogen makes up about 78% of the air.

327. Organic chemistry is the chemistry of carbon compounds.

328. The current in the conductor causes a magnetic field.

316.　このバッテリーは、5時間の連続使用が可能だ。

317.　他の惑星に行くには、宇宙空間を通らなければならない。

318.　合金は単一の金属にない特性を持っていることがある。

319.　化学反応では物質の増減はない。

320.　潤滑によって機械の運転は滑らかで静かになる。

321.　その会社は、毎年いくつかの新製品を売り出している。

322.　この数の1/4を見つけるには、それを4で割ればよい。

323.　気体は一般に液体や固体よりも軽い。

324.　氷が水に変わると体積はいくらか減る。

325.　7mと1mの割合は7：1か7/1のように書く。

326.　窒素の空気に占める割合は約78%である。

327.　有機化学は炭素化合物の化学である。

328.　導体の電流によって磁界ができる。

329. An unbalanced load can cause the shaft to vibrate.

330. A lens bends a ray of light passing through it.

331. When ignited, a combustible mixture expands rapidly.

332. Dirt or other impurities will decrease engine efficiency.

333. Machines have a one-year guarantee against breakdowns.

334. Do not put this type of plastic too close to the fire, or it will melt.

335. Most chemical reactions are accompanied by a thermal change.

336. A Bunsen burner is a gas burner with a very hot flame.

337. The volume of a gas increases as the temperature rises.

338. Personal computers are very helpful in our daily jobs.

339. Steel is a good conductor of electricity, as are most metals.

340. Filtration is an operation to separate solids from liquids.

341. Turn the switch off before taking the plug out of the socket.

329.　シャフトの荷重が釣り合っていないと振動の原因になる。

330.　レンズはそれを通る光線を屈折させる。

331.　可燃性の混合気は火をつけると急速に膨脹する。

332.　ごみや不純物があると、エンジン効率が下がる。

333.　機械の故障に対して1年間の保証が付いている。

334.　この種のプラスチックは火気に近づけ過ぎないこと、さもなければ融ける。

335.　ほとんどの化学反応は熱の変化を伴う。

336.　ブンゼンバーナーは高温の炎を出すガスバーナーである。

337.　気体の体積は、温度の上昇とともに大きくなる。

338.　パソコンは、日常の仕事をする上で、大変便利である。

339.　たいていの金属と同様に、鋼鉄は電気をよく通す。

340.　濾過とは、液体から固体を分離する操作のことである。

341.　スイッチを切った後、コンセントからプラグを抜きなさい。

342. There are various ways of lowering the temperature.

343. Sugar dissolves faster in warm water than in cold water.

344. A straight line is the shortest distance between two points.

345. If a plastic pipe is used, rust prevention will be unnecessary.

346. Impurities are eliminated by passing the liquid through a filter.

347. Triangles are plane figures with three straight sides.

348. I have just finished testing the performance of this tuner.

349. More fuel is needed as the speed increases.

350. A broadcasting station transmits television and radio programs.

351. A rise in temperature causes the column of mercury to rise.

352. This computer works four times as fast as the previous ones.

353. Lead resists attack by corrosive substances.

354. Great heat is released when hydrogen and carbon are burned.

342. 温度を下げるためには、いろいろな方法がある。

343. 砂糖は冷水よりも温水に早く溶ける。

344. 直線は2点間の最短距離である。

345. プラスチック製のパイプを使えば、錆び止めの必要がなくなる。

346. 不純物は、その液体をフィルターに通すことによって除去される。

347. 三角形は3つの辺からできている平面図形である。

348. 私はこのチューナーの性能テストを終えたばかりである。

349. スピードが上がるにつれて燃料の消費量は増える。

350. 放送局はテレビ番組とラジオ番組を流す。

351. 温度が上昇すると水銀柱が上がる。

352. このコンピュータは従来の4倍の速さで作動する。

353. 鉛は腐蝕物質の浸食に耐える。

354. 水素と炭素が燃焼すると大量の熱が出る。

355. The center line passes through the center of a body.

356. The diameter is less than one third of the circumference.

357. Use the proper tools. Otherwise an accident may occur.

358. The computer language is called machine language.

359. Pushing this button resets the display to all zeros.

360. The amount of energy packed in a substance is constant.

361. Precautions must be followed to prevent injuries.

362. The temperature of the water is read at two-minute intervals.

363. If the radius of a circle is 2 cm, the area is about 12.6 cm².

364. Tin is so soft that it can be rolled into very thin sheets.

365. The plate is coated with fluorescent paint.

366. The higher the altitude, the less dense the air.

367. White reflects more light than black.

368. Such phenomena rarely occur.

355.　中心線は物体の中心を通っている。

356.　直径は円周の1／3未満である。

357.　適切な工具を使いなさい。そうしないと事故が起こることがある。

358.　コンピュータ言語は、機械言語と呼ばれている。

359.　このボタンを押すと、表示はすべて0にリセットされる。

360.　物質に蓄えられるエネルギー量は、一定である。

361.　けがを防ぐには注意事項を守らなければならない。

362.　水温は2分おきに読みとられる。

363.　円の半径が2㎝の場合、面積は約12.6㎠になる。

364.　錫はきわめてやわらかいので、非常に薄いシート状に延ばせる。

365.　プレートには螢光塗料が塗ってある。

366.　高いところに行けば行くほど、空気は薄くなる。

367.　白は黒よりも光を反射する。

368.　そのような現象はめったに起こらない。

369. Combustion was incomplete because of insufficient oxygen.

370. Whenever possible, put the instruction manual next to the machine.

371. Gravity is the natural pull toward the center of the earth.

372. The change from solid to liquid is known as melting.

373. Show the relation between A and B in a diagram.

374. Analysis showed that it contained harmful substances.

375. A thorough inspection is made here.

376. If the current is too large, the fuse melts and cuts off the current.

377. Thirst is the sensation that warns us that the body needs water.

378. The number of revolutions depends on the type of generator.

379. The computer itself is a machine, so computers do break down and have failures.

380. The vapor pressure of a liquid increases as the temperature rises.

381. An electric fan is used to make people cooler, not to cool the air.

369.　酸素不足のため不完全燃焼となった。

370.　取扱説明書は、できるだけ機械のそばに置きなさい。

371.　重力とは、地球の中心に向かう自然の引力のことである。

372.　固体から液体に変わることを溶解という。

373.　ＡとＢの関係を図に表しなさい。

374.　分析の結果、有害物質が含まれていることが分かった。

375.　ここでは入念な検査が行われている。

376.　過大な電流が通ると、ヒューズが溶けて、回路を切る。

377.　喉の渇きは、人体に水が足りないことを訴える感覚である。

378.　発電機の回転数は機種によって違う。

379.　コンピュータは本来、機械であるから、故障もするし誤動作もする。

380.　液体の蒸気圧は、温度の上昇とともに高くなる。

381.　扇風機は人を涼しくするもので、空気を冷やすものでない。

382. Compute the required thickness of the concrete from this formula.

383. Direct current is defined as current that flows in one direction.

384. These two transistor radios are similar in shape but different in price.

385. A microscope makes it possible for us to see very small things.

386. The programmer must decide what programming language to use.

387. Non-corroding materials are used in this part.

388. The resistance of a conductor increases in proportion to its length.

389. Franklin proved by a dangerous experiment that lightning is electricity.

390. This antenna is small and light for easy portability.

391. Mercury contained in dissolved metals can be extracted from them by distillation.

392. New machinery can greatly increase production.

393. The analysis of these methods will appear in the latter part of the book.

382.　この式から、必要なコンクリートの厚さを
　　　導きなさい。

383.　直流は一方向に流れる電流と定義される。

384.　この２つのトランジスタラジオは、形は似
　　　ているが値段が違う。

385.　顕微鏡によって、微小な物を見ることがで
　　　きる。

386.　プログラマは、使用するプログラム言語を
　　　決める必要がある。

387.　この部分には、腐食しない材料が使われて
　　　いる。

388.　導体の抵抗は長さに比例して増える。

389.　フランクリンは危険な実験により、稲妻が
　　　電気であることを証明した。

390.　このアンテナは、持ち運びが楽なように小
　　　型軽量にしてある。

391.　溶解した金属に含まれている水銀は、蒸留
　　　することによって抽出できる。

392.　新しい機械の導入で生産は飛躍的に伸びる。

393.　これらの方法の分析内容は、その本の後半
　　　に出てくる。

394. The velocity of a liquid flowing under constant pressure depends on the diameter of the pipe.

395. There are two ways of connecting resistors: serial and parallel.

396. Nearly one tenth of industrial accidents are caused by the misuse of hand tools.

397. Jacks are used for raising and lowering loads, not for supporting them.

398. The atmosphere contains various gases, including oxygen and carbon dioxide.

399. Glass, nylon, and rubber are very poor conductors of electricity and heat.

400. Detergent molecules reduce the surface tension of a drop of water.

401. This instrument can be used anywhere because it has no power cord.

402. Turnover fell short of the targeted amount.

403. Planing will reduce the friction between two rough boards.

404. Among the engines exhibited here, this one has the greatest power output.

405. The melting point is the temperature at which a solid becomes a liquid.

394.　液体の流れの速度は、一定の圧力下ではパイプの直径による。

395.　抵抗を接続する方法には直列と並列がある。

396.　工業関係の事故のほぼ1/10は、手工具の誤用によるものである。

397.　ジャッキは荷物を支えるためでなく、それらを上げたり下げたりするために使われる。

398.　大気には、酸素や炭酸ガスをはじめ、いろいろなガスが含まれている。

399.　ガラス、ナイロン、ゴムは電気および熱の伝導性が大変低い物質である。

400.　洗剤の分子は水滴の表面張力を減少させる。

401.　この装置には電源コードがないので、どこででも使える。

402.　売上高は目標額を下回った。

403.　ざらざらしている2枚の板の表面を削ると、摩擦が少なくなる。

404.　このエンジンは、ここに展示されているエンジンの中で最大の出力がある。

405.　融点とは固体が液体に変わる温度のことである。

406. Two objects which have the same electrical charge repel each other.

407. This filter can remove as much as 99 percent of the dust from the air.

408. It's very cold. The temperature is below zero.

409. Copper, a reddish metal, is an excellent conductor of electricity.

410. The area of a room 3 meters wide by 3 meters long is 9 square meters.

411. The gasoline-and-air mixture is drawn into the cylinder, compressed, and ignited by a spark.

412. The wire between the two terminals should be slightly slack.

413. Light rays passing through a convex lens are refracted and converge at one point.

414. The rate of operation of this machine is better than the previous one.

415. If the device fails to operate properly, consult your manual.

416. The heart is a kind of natural pump that circulates the blood throughout the body.

417. The earth is surrounded by a mixture of gases called the atmosphere.

406.　同じ電荷を帯びている２つの物体は反発し合う。

407.　このフィルターは空気中のゴミを99％も取り除く。

408.　たいへん寒い。気温は零下だ。

409.　銅は、赤みがかった金属で電気をよく通す。

410.　縦・横３ｍの部屋の面積は９㎡である。

411.　ガソリンと空気の混合気は、シリンダに送られ、圧縮され、火花によって点火される。

412.　両端子間の線は、少しゆるめにしておきなさい。

413.　凸レンズを通った光線は、屈折し１点に集まる。

414.　この機械の稼働率は前のものより良い。

415.　装置が適切に作動しないようであればマニュアルを見なさい。

416.　心臓は、体内で血液を循環させる一種の自然のポンプである。

417.　地球は大気という気体の混合物で覆われている。

418. A farsighted person can see things far away better than things up close.

419. Fuse wire is made from a material with a lower melting point than copper.

420. A triangle has three sides and three angles.

421. Detergent molecules reduce the surface tension of water.

422. The more concentrated the reducing agent, the stronger its reducing power.

423. When iodine crystals are heated to 114℃, they melt, forming liquid iodine.

424. The circumference of a circle is 3.14 times as long as the diameter.

425. One calorie is the amount of heat required to raise the temperature of one gram of water 1℃.

426. A microscope magnifies things too small to be seen with the naked eye.

427. The colored band formed when light passes through a prism is called a spectrum.

428. As you put more air into the tire, the pressure increases and the tire gets harder.

429. The boiling point is one of the most important physical constants of a substance.

418.　遠視の人は近いものより、遠いものの方が
よく見える。

419.　ヒューズは銅よりも融点が低い物質ででき
ている。

420.　三角形は、3つの辺と3つの角からできて
いる。

421.　洗剤の分子は水の表面張力を弱める。

422.　還元剤は濃縮されているほど還元力は強く
なる。

423.　ヨウ素の結晶を114℃まで熱すると、溶解
して液体ヨウ素になる。

424.　円周は直径の3.14倍である。

425.　1カロリーとは、水1gの温度を1℃上げ
るのに要する熱量をいう。

426.　顕微鏡は、肉眼では見えない小さなものを
拡大する。

427.　光がプリズムを通ってできる色のついたバ
ンドをスペクトルという。

428.　空気を入れれば入れるほど圧力は上がり、
タイヤは硬くなってくる。

429.　沸点は物質の物理学上の重要な定数の一つ
である。

430.　A computer should be installed in a dustfree, air-conditioned room.

431.　A plane mirror reflects an identical image with its sides reversed.

432.　A manual transmission is easier to maintain than an automatic transmission.

433.　The larger the number of samples, the less the possibility of experimental error.

434.　One watt is the power of a circuit in which one ampere is flowing under a voltage of one volt.

435.　The introductory remarks on page 1 explain how the manual should be used.

436.　The combustion processes in the gasoline engine and the diesel engine differ significantly.

437.　There are two kinds of electric charge, which, for convenience, are called positive and negative.

438.　One form of energy can be transformed into another form of energy under a variety of conditions.

439.　Heat can be transferred from one body to another in three ways: by conduction, by convection, or by radiation.

440.　Exhaust gases from a diesel engine consist chiefly of carbon dioxide, water vapor, oxygen, and nitrogen.

430. コンピュータは、ほこりのない空調装置のある部屋に設置されるべきである。

431. 平面鏡は左右が反対の同じ像を映す。

432. 手動変速機は自動変速機よりも保守が簡単である。

433. サンプル数が多いほど、実験の誤差の生じる可能性は少ない。

434. 1ワットとは、1ボルトの電圧のもとで1アンペアが流れる回路内での力である。

435. 1ページの序文にはマニュアルの使用法が述べられている。

436. ガソリンエンジンとディーゼルエンジンの燃焼工程は著しく異なる。

437. 電荷には2種類ある。便宜上、プラス（正）とマイナス（負）と呼んでいる。

438. ある形のエネルギーは、いろいろな条件によって違った形のエネルギーに変換される。

439. 熱を物体間で伝えるには、伝導、対流、輻射の3通りがある。

440. ディーゼルエンジンの排気は、主に二酸化炭素、水蒸気、酸素、窒素から成っている。

441.　The calculations were so complicated that they could not be done without a computer.

442.　Whenever one surface moves over another, a force resisting the movement is produced.

443.　A beam of light from a searchlight or car headlight appears to travel straight. This fact can be ascertained by conducting a simple experiment.

444.　The volt, the ampere, and the ohm are the three fundamental units of measurement in electricity.

445.　A rocket carries its own supply of oxygen to burn the fuel, but a jet takes in air and compresses it during flight.

446.　To convert Fahrenheit temperatures (°F) to Celsius temperatures (°C), the following formula is used:
$$°C = \frac{5}{9} (°F - 32)$$

447.　The volume of a gas is constant if the temperature and the pressure do not change.

448.　When salt water is heated, the salt is left as a deposit after the water has changed to steam.

449.　Mixing metallic elements forms a new kind of metallic substance called an alloy.

441.　計算が非常に複雑なので、コンピュータを使わざるを得なかった。

442.　1つの面がもう1つの面上を動くときはいつでも、その動きに抵抗する力が生じる。

443.　探照灯や自動車のヘッドライトから出る光線は、直進するように見える。このことは簡単な実験をやってみるとわかる。

444.　ボルト、アンペア、オームは電気の3つの基本測定単位である。

445.　ロケットは、燃料を燃やすためにロケット自身に必要な酸素を運んでいくが、一方、ジェットでは飛行中に空気を吸入、圧縮する。

446.　華氏の温度を摂氏に変えるには、次の公式が使われる。
$$\text{℃} = \frac{5}{9}(\text{℉} - 32)$$

447.　気体の体積は温度と圧力が変化しなければ一定である。

448.　食塩水が熱せられると水は蒸気に変わり、後に塩分が沈澱物として残る。

449.　金属元素を混ぜ合わせると合金という新しい金属物質が作られる。

450.　Chemical reaction is a process that converts substances into other substances.

451.　Density is calculated by dividing mass by volume.

452.　Integrated circuits make it possible to produce small size calculators.

453.　The high surface temperature is caused by the massive greenhouse effect of carbon dioxide.

454.　When a certain temperature is reached, the substance, if pure, melts suddenly.

455.　The resistance of a conductor decreases as the area of its cross section increases.

456.　Don't oil, clean, adjust, or repair any machine while it is running.

457.　Iron containing a small amount of carbon can be magnetized by placing the iron in contact with a magnet.

458.　Be sure to close the lid when the temperature reaches 200℃.

459.　A thin film of oil keeps the bearing from corroding.

460.　A rough tooth surface causes high wear.

461.　You will find Ohm's law useful when learning about electricity.

450. 化学反応とは、ある物質を他の物質に変える過程のことである。

451. 密度は質量を体積で割って求める。

452. 集積回路のおかげで、小型の計算機を作ることができる。

453. 二酸化炭素による巨大な温室効果のために、地表の温度は高くなる。

454. この物質は不純物を含まない場合には、ある一定温度で急激に融解する。

455. 導体の抵抗は、その断面積が増せば小さくなる。

456. 機械が作動中は、給油、掃除、調節あるいは修理をしてはならない。

457. 少量の炭素を含んだ鉄は、磁石に接触させておくと磁性を帯びてくる。

458. 測定が200℃になったら、必ず蓋を閉めなさい。

459. 薄い油膜のためにベアリングはさびない。

460. 歯車の表面がざらざらしていると摩耗が激しい。

461. 電気のことを学ぶときには、オームの法則が役に立つ。

462.　Many rats have developed what is called "immunity" to some poisons.

463.　You have only to set up posts at intervals of 1.8 meters.

464.　Tie the package tightly to keep it from loosening.

465.　Similar results are expected from the current tests.

466.　The hole is too small in diameter and too deep to be measured by this gauge.

467.　Vaccines protect our bodies by speeding the production of substances called antibodies.

468.　If there are problems, the system can diagnose and correct them automatically.

469.　Liquefied natural gas is attracting more attention as a low-pollution electric power fuel.

470.　The viscosity of a liquid decreases as the temperature rises.

471.　The probability of damage is not great enough to worry about.

472.　Stop the machine and lock the power switch in the OFF position.

473.　Refer to the following manuals for maintenance instructions.

474.　Perform a complete daily inspection.

462.　ある毒に対して、いわゆる「免疫」を持っているネズミが多い。

463.　1.8mの間隔で柱を立てさえすればよい。

464.　ほどけないように小包をしっかり縛ってください。

465.　現在行われているテストから、同様な結果がでるものと期待されている。

466.　この穴は直径が小さく深すぎるので、このゲージでは測定できない。

467.　ワクチンは、抗体と呼ばれる物質の製造を早める働きによってわれわれの体を守る。

468.　たとえ問題が起こったとしても、このシステムは自動的に問題箇所を発見し、修正する。

469.　液化天然ガスは、環境汚染の少ない電力用燃料としてますます注目を集めている。

470.　液体の粘性は温度が上昇するにつれて減少する。

471.　損傷の可能性は心配するほど大きいものではない。

472.　機械を止め、電源スイッチをオフの位置に固定しなさい。

473.　整備要領については、下記のマニュアルを参照しなさい。

474.　毎日の点検を完全に実施すること。

475. Hard water is unsuitable for household use because it requires so much soap.

476. Return damaged, unusable coolers to the manufacturer.

477. We cannot continue to rely on coal, oil, and gas in the future as much as we have in the past.

478. The expansion rate of iron is constant regardless of temperature.

479. An error in these settings will cause incorrect data to be sent to or received from the computer.

480. The electrical properties of semiconductors depend very much on their purity.

481. A spark ignites the fuel in the cylinder, and the expansion caused by combustion drives the piston.

482. Arithmetical operations include addition, subtraction, multiplication, and division.

483. A relief valve is provided to protect the pump from excessive pressure.

484. Communication satellites are most economical when they operate twenty-four hours a day.

485. Install the ventilating fan close to the ceiling; the higher the better.

475.　硬水は、多量の石鹸を必要とするので、家庭用には適さない。

476.　損傷して使えない冷却器は、メーカーに返却しなさい。

477.　私たちは、石炭、石油、ガスにこれまでと同じようにいつまでも依存し続けることはできない。

478.　鉄の膨脹率は温度の高低に関係なく一定である。

479.　この設定を一つでも誤ると、不正確なデータを計算機に送ったり出力させることになる。

480.　半導体の電気特性は、その純度に応じて大きな違いが出る。

481.　火花がシリンダの中の燃料に点火し、燃焼による膨脹がピストンを動かす。

482.　算術計算には加減乗除がある。

483.　ポンプを過剰圧力から保護するため、リリーフ弁が設置されている。

484.　通信衛星は、1日24時間稼動する場合に最も経済効率が良い。

485.　換気扇を天井の近くに取り付けなさい。高いところほどよい。

486.　Once a body is in motion, it tends to continue in motion unless acted on by an external force.

487.　Rapid cooling produces irregular contractions, which weaken the metal.

488.　A shape memory alloy is a metal that can be deformed when cooled but returns to its original shape when heated.

489.　An electron carries a negative charge and an atomic nucleus carries a positive charge.

490.　The characteristics of a material are its strength and its resistance to stress, wear, and bending.

491.　The figure 4.38 rounded to one decimal place is 4.4.

492.　Parts exceeding the allowable wear limit must be replaced.

493.　A large difference in temperature causes cracks on the painted surface.

494.　This material is too brittle to endure thermal and vibrational shock.

495.　A robot is equipped with sensors to detect the objects on which it operates.

496.　Liquids and gases are made up of tiny, constantly moving particles called molecules.

497.　An overspeed alarm function is included to avoid false measurement.

486. 物体はいったん動き始めると、外力が加えられない限り運動し続けようとする。

487. 金属を急速に冷却すると不規則な収縮が生じ、これが金属を弱化させる。

488. 形状記憶合金とは冷却した場合に変形し、加熱すると、もとに戻る金属である。

489. 電子はマイナスの電荷を持ち、原子核はプラスの電荷を持つ。

490. 材料の特性には、強さや応力、摩耗、曲げなどに対する抵抗がある。

491. 4.38を、小数点以下第2位で四捨五入する（まるめて小数第1位にする）と4.4になる。

492. 許容摩耗限界値を超えた部品は交換しなければならない。

493. 温度の差が激しいと塗装面にひびが入る。

494. この材料はもろすぎて、熱や振動のショックに耐えられない。

495. ロボットには、操作する対象物を検知するためのセンサが装備されている。

496. 液体や気体は、分子という絶え間なく運動している小さな粒子で構成されている。

497. 誤測定を防ぐために、オーバースピード警報機能が内蔵されている。

498. Further investigation revealed that the periodic change was caused by a faulty piece of equipment.

499. Transistors were used wherever efficient amplification was required in a small space.

500. The higher the rate of liquid flow, the greater the risk of turbulence.

498.　さらに調べると、周期的に現れる変化は装
　　　置の一部の不良によることが明らかになった。

499.　トランジスタは、場所は狭いが増幅の効率
　　　を高めたい場合には必ず使われた。

500.　液体の速度が速くなるにつれて、乱流の生
　　　じるおそれが高くなる。

基礎単語　1600

A

☐ abbreviation	短縮（形）
☐ above-mentioned	上記の
☐ absolute temperature	絶対温度
☐ absorption	吸収
☐ abstract	摘要
☐ abundance	豊富
☐ abundantly	豊富に
☐ abuse	誤用
☐ acceleration	加速度
☐ accelerator	アクセル
☐ accessory	付属物
☐ accidental	偶然の
☐ accompanying	伴う
☐ accumulate	蓄積する
☐ accuracy	精度
☐ acetic acid	酢酸
☐ acid	酸／酸性の
☐ acquirement	獲得
☐ act	作用する／動く
☐ action	作用
☐ activate	活性化する
☐ active carbon	活性炭
☐ active volcano	活火山
☐ acute	鋭角の／急性の
☐ adapt	適応させる
☐ addition	付加
☐ adequate	十分な
☐ adhere	固執する
☐ adhesive agents	接着剤
☐ adhesives	接着剤

☐	adjacent	隣接の
☐	adjoining	隣り合わせの
☐	adjust	調整する
☐	adjustment	調整
☐	admissible	許容の
☐	advance notice	事前通告
☐	advanced	進歩した
☐	advantage	優利さ
☐	affinity	親和力
☐	affirmative	肯定的な
☐	affix	添付する
☐	aggravate	悪化させる
☐	aid	援助
☐	air inlet cam	吸気カム
☐	air pollution	大気汚染
☐	air-cooled engine	空冷エンジン
☐	aircraft	航空機
☐	alarm	警報（器）
☐	alchemy	錬金術
☐	alcohol	アルコール
☐	alignment	一直線にすること
☐	alkaline	アルカリ性の
☐	alloy	合金
☐	alternate	変更する
☐	alternating current	交流
☐	alternative	二者択一の
☐	alternator	交流発電機
☐	aluminum	アルミニウム
☐	amendment	修正
☐	ammeter	電流計
☐	amount	量
☐	amperage	アンペア数

☐	amplifier	増幅器／アンプ
☐	amplitude	振幅
☐	analogy	相似
☐	analysis	分析
☐	angle	角度
☐	angle steel	形鋼
☐	animal experiment	動物実験
☐	anion	陰イオン
☐	anneal	焼きなます
☐	annual sum	年額
☐	anode	陽極
☐	antecedent	先行する
☐	anti-rust solution	さび止め液
☐	anti-spoilage	防腐剤
☐	antibiotics	抗生物質
☐	apex	頂点
☐	apparatus	装置
☐	apparent	明らかな
☐	appendix	付録
☐	applicable	適用できる
☐	application	応用
☐	apply	加える
☐	appraise	見積もる／評価する
☐	appreciably	かなり
☐	appreciate	賞賛する／価値を上げる
☐	apprentice	見習い
☐	appropriate	適切な
☐	approval	承認
☐	approximate	概算の
☐	apt to ～	～しやすい

☐	arbitrary	任意の
☐	arbitrator	仲裁人
☐	area	面積
☐	arithmetic device	演算装置
☐	aromatic	芳香族の
☐	arrange	並べる／整える
☐	arrangement	配置／配列
☐	array	配列
☐	artery	動脈
☐	artificial	人工の
☐	as of ～	～現在（で）
☐	as shown in ～	～に示す通り
☐	assembly	組み立て
☐	assets	資産
☐	assignment	割り当て ／権利の譲渡
☐	assimilate	吸収する
☐	assimilation	同化
☐	assume	推測する
☐	assumption	仮定
☐	astronaut	宇宙飛行士
☐	astronomer	天文学者
☐	atmosphere	大気
☐	atmospheric pressure	気圧
☐	atomic nucleus	原子核
☐	attachment	付属品
☐	attainable	到達できる
☐	attainment	達成
☐	attribute	属性
☐	automatic control	自動制御
☐	automobile	自動車
☐	automotive mechanics	自動車工学

☐	auxiliary	補助の
☐	available	入手できる
☐	avoidable	回避できる
☐	axial	軸の
☐	axis	軸
☐	axle	車軸
☐	axle lathe	普通旋盤

B

☐	backwards	後方に
☐	bacteria	細菌
☐	balance	秤
☐	ball-peen hammer	丸頭ハンマ
☐	balloon-borne	気球搭載の
☐	bar chart	棒グラフ
☐	barrier	障壁
☐	base	塩基
☐	base line	基線
☐	batch processing	バッチ処理
☐	battery	電池
☐	battery plate	極板
☐	beam	梁/光線
☐	below ～	～以下
☐	beneficial	有益な
☐	bent	曲がった
☐	biennial	隔年の
☐	binary system	二進法
☐	binocular	双眼鏡
☐	biology	生物学
☐	blade	刃
☐	blast furnace	溶鉱炉

☐	blood pressure	血圧
☐	blueprint	青写真
☐	body	本体
☐	boiling point	沸点
☐	boost	増加／上昇
☐	bordering	接している
☐	boring	穴あけ ／ボーリング
☐	botany	植物学
☐	bottom	底部
☐	boundary	境界
☐	brain death	脳死
☐	braking	制動
☐	brass	真鍮
☐	breach	違反
☐	breadth	幅
☐	breakdown	故障
☐	briefly	手短かに
☐	brittle	もろい
☐	broken	故障した
☐	bronze	青銅
☐	broom	ほうき
☐	build-up	堆積
☐	bulkhead	遮断壁
☐	bulldozer	ブルドーザー
☐	burst	爆発
☐	button	ボタン

C

☐	calculation	計算
☐	caliber	口径

☐	calibrate	目盛る
☐	calibration	目盛り
☐	cancellation	（契約の）解除
☐	capability	能力
☐	capable	可能な
☐	capacitance	静電容量
☐	capacity	容量／能力
☐	capsule	カプセル
☐	caption	表題／解説
☐	carbohydrate	炭水化物
☐	carbon	炭素
☐	carbon dioxide	二酸化炭素
☐	carbon monoxide	一酸化炭素
☐	carburetor	気化器
☐	cardboard	厚紙／ボール紙
☐	cast	鋳造する
☐	catalysis	触媒作用
☐	catalyzer	触媒
☐	cathode	陰極
☐	cation	陽イオン
☐	causal relation	因果関係
☐	cause	原因
☐	cease	止まる
☐	cell	電池／細胞
☐	cellophane	セロファン
☐	center	中心
☐	center of gravity	重心
☐	centigrade	摂氏
☐	centrifugal force	遠心力
☐	chain reaction	連鎖反応
☐	chamber	室
☐	change gear	変速装置

☐	changeover	切り換え
☐	charge	充電
☐	chemical change	化学変化
☐	chemical equilibrium	化学平衡
☐	chemicals	化学薬品
☐	chimney	煙突
☐	chip	細片
☐	chisel	のみ／たがね／チゼル
☐	chlorine	塩素
☐	chromium	クロム
☐	chronic	慢性の
☐	circle	円
☐	circuit	回路
☐	circuit breaker	遮断器
☐	circuit diagram	回路図
☐	circulation	循環
☐	circumference	円周
☐	circumstance	状況
☐	civil engineering	土木工学
☐	clarify	明らかにする
☐	classify	分類する
☐	clay	粘土
☐	clean	きれいにする
☐	clear	明確な
☐	clip	止め具
☐	clockwise	右回り／時計方向
☐	clockwork	時計仕掛け
☐	close	（回路を）閉じる
☐	coal	石炭
☐	coarse	粗い
☐	coat	被覆する

☐ code	符号
☐ coefficient	係数
☐ cohesion	粘着力
☐ coincide	一致する
☐ collide	衝突する
☐ collision	衝突
☐ column	柱
☐ combustible	可燃性の
☐ combustion	燃焼
☐ come into effect	効力を生ずる
☐ commercial	市販の
☐ commodity	商品
☐ comparison	比較
☐ compartment	仕切り
☐ compatible	互換性の
☐ compensation	補償
☐ competitive	競合できる
☐ complementary	補足的な
☐ complete	完全な
☐ complex	複雑な
☐ component	部品
☐ composition	組成
☐ compound	化合物
☐ compress	圧縮する
☐ compressed air	圧縮空気
☐ compression	圧縮
☐ compressor	コンプレッサ
☐ comprise	含む／〜から成る
☐ compute	計算する
☐ concave lens	凹レンズ
☐ concentration	濃度
☐ concerned	当該の

☐	conclusion	結論
☐	conclusive	決定的な
☐	concrete	具体的な
☐	condensation	凝縮
☐	condense	凝縮する
☐	condition	状態
☐	conduction	伝導
☐	conductivity	伝導率
☐	conductor	伝導体
☐	conduit	導管
☐	cone	円錐
☐	confidential	秘密の
☐	configuration	配列
☐	conflict	矛盾する
☐	consecutive	連続の
☐	consequence	結果
☐	conservation	保存
☐	considerable	かなりの／考慮すべき
☐	consist of ～	～から成る
☐	consistency	一貫性
☐	consistent	一貫した
☐	consolidation	合併
☐	conspicuous	目立つ
☐	constant	定数／一定の
☐	constituent	構成要素
☐	constitute	構成する
☐	consume	消費する
☐	consumption	消費
☐	contain	内蔵する
☐	container	コンテナ
☐	contaminate	汚染する

☐	contemplate	考察する
☐	content(s)	含有量
☐	continual	連続的な
☐	continuous	絶え間ない
☐	contract	契約
☐	contract	収縮する
☐	contraction	収縮
☐	contradict	矛盾する
☐	contrary	相反する
☐	control panel	制御盤
☐	control valve	制御弁
☐	convection	対流
☐	conventional	従来の
☐	conversion	変換
☐	convert	転換する／変換する
☐	convex lens	凸レンズ
☐	convincing	説得力のある
☐	cool	冷却する
☐	coolant	冷却剤
☐	cooling	冷却
☐	copper	銅
☐	cord	コード
☐	core	核
☐	correlate	相関させる
☐	correlation	相関
☐	correspond	一致する
☐	corresponding	対応する
☐	corrosion	腐蝕
☐	corrosive	腐蝕性の
☐	cost	費用
☐	costly	高価な

☐	counterclockwise	左回り /反時計方向
☐	crack	割れ
☐	crating	梱包
☐	criterion	基準
☐	critical	臨界の／致命的な
☐	critical temperature	臨界温度
☐	cross section	断面（図）
☐	cross-sectional area	断面積
☐	crude oil	原油
☐	cruising speed	巡航速度
☐	crystal	結晶
☐	crystalline	結晶（性）の
☐	cube	立方体
☐	cubic meter	立方メートル
☐	current (flow)	電流
☐	curved line	曲線
☐	cycle	周期
☐	cylinder	シリンダ

D

☐	darken	暗くする
☐	data processing	データ処理
☐	deal with	取り扱う
☐	decade	10年間
☐	decagon	十角形
☐	decay	腐敗
☐	decimal	十進法の
☐	decimal point	小数点
☐	decompose	分解する
☐	decrease	減少する

☐	default	不履行
☐	defect	欠陥
☐	defective	故障している
☐	defective car	欠陥車
☐	deficiency	不足
☐	definition	定義
☐	deflect	偏向させる
☐	deformation	変形
☐	degrade	低下させる／退化する
☐	delay	遅延
☐	delivery	引き渡し
☐	demand	需要（量）
☐	density	密度
☐	depict	描写する
☐	depollute	汚染を除去する
☐	depot	デポ／倉庫
☐	depreciate	低下させる／切り下げる
☐	deprive	奪う
☐	depth	深さ
☐	derivative	誘導体
☐	designate	表示する
☐	designation	呼び名
☐	desired value	期待値
☐	destruction	破壊
☐	destructive	破壊的な
☐	detail	詳細
☐	detailed	詳細な
☐	detect	検出する
☐	detector	検出器
☐	detergent	洗剤

☐	deteriorate	悪化する／価値が下がる
☐	deterioration	悪化
☐	determine	測定する／規定する
☐	detonate	爆発する
☐	develop	開発する
☐	development	開発
☐	device	装置
☐	dewpoint	露点
☐	diagnosis	診断
☐	diagram	図／図表
☐	diameter	直径
☐	diffraction	回折
☐	diffusion	拡散
☐	dig	掘る
☐	dilution	希釈
☐	dimensions	寸法
☐	diminish	減少させる
☐	dip	浸す
☐	direct current	直流
☐	direction	方向／指示
☐	dirt	汚れ
☐	disassemble	分解する
☐	disassembly	分解
☐	discernible	識別できる
☐	discharge	放電する
☐	discharge tube	放電管
☐	disconnect	接続を断つ
☐	discontinuity	不連続
☐	discontinuous	連続しない
☐	discrete	分離している

☐	discretely	個別的に
☐	dispersion	分散
☐	displacement	排気量／変位
☐	display	示す
☐	dispose of	処理する
☐	disseminate	拡散させる
☐	dissociate	解離する
☐	dissociation	解離
☐	dissolve	溶かす
☐	distance	距離
☐	distill	蒸留する
☐	distillation	蒸留
☐	distilled water	蒸留水
☐	distinct	明瞭な／判明な
☐	distortion	ひずみ／ゆがみ
☐	distribution	分布／配分
☐	diverse	異なる種類の
☐	domestic	国産の
☐	dominant	支配的な
☐	dormant volcano	休火山
☐	dotted line	点線
☐	downward	下方へ
☐	drain	排水（管）
☐	drainage	排水
☐	drastically	大幅に
☐	draw	吸気する／（線）を引く
☐	drawing	図面
☐	drilling	穴あけ
☐	drilling machine	ボール盤
☐	drive shaft	駆動軸
☐	drycell	乾電池

☐	ductile	展性のある
☐	ductility	延性
☐	duplicating machine	複写機
☐	durability	耐久力
☐	durable	耐久性の
☐	duralumin	ジュラルミン
☐	duration	継続／期間
☐	dust	微粒子／ほこり

E

☐	earthquake	地震
☐	ecology	生態学
☐	economic consideration	経済性
☐	economical	経済的な
☐	eddy current	うず電流
☐	edge welding	ヘリ溶接
☐	effect	効果
☐	effective value	実効値
☐	effectively	効果的に
☐	efficient curve	効率曲線
☐	elastic	弾性の
☐	elasticity	弾性
☐	electric charge	電荷
☐	electric heat	電熱
☐	electricity	電気
☐	electrode	電極
☐	electron	電子
☐	element	要素／元素
☐	eliminate	取り除く
☐	elimination	除去
☐	emerge	出現する

☐	emergency	緊急
☐	emergency equipment	非常装置
☐	emission	放射
☐	emission standard	排ガス規制基準
☐	emissive	放射性のある
☐	emit	発する
☐	empty	空の
☐	enclose	囲う
☐	endurance	持続
☐	energy	エネルギー
☐	energy-saving	エネルギー節約の
☐	enhance	高める
☐	enriched uranium	濃縮ウラン
☐	entail	結果として伴う
☐	enumerated in ～	～に列挙されている
☐	environment	環境
☐	environment standards	環境基準
☐	enzyme	酵素
☐	epidemic	流行性の
☐	equation	方程式
☐	equilibrium	平衡
☐	equip	設備する／取り付ける
☐	equipment	装置
☐	equipped	装備した
☐	equivalent	当量
☐	error	誤差
☐	error-free	間違いのない
☐	eruption	噴火
☐	escape	漏出
☐	estimate	見積もり

☐ evacuate	空にする
☐ evaporate	蒸発する
☐ evaporation	蒸発
☐ even number	偶数
☐ eventually	結局は
☐ evidence	根拠
☐ evident	明らかな
☐ evolve	（理論を）展開する
☐ exact	正確な
☐ examine	調べる
☐ exceed	超える
☐ exclusive switch	専用スイッチ
☐ execution of duties	任務の遂行
☐ exert	作用を及ぼす
☐ exhale	（息を）吐く／発散する
☐ exhaust	排気
☐ exhaust gas	排（気）ガス
☐ exhaust valve	排気バルブ
☐ existent	現存の
☐ expansion	膨脹
☐ expansion bend	伸縮ベンド
☐ expansion coil	伸縮コイル
☐ expectation	期待（値）
☐ expected	期待通りの
☐ expenditure	支出
☐ expenses	費用
☐ experienced	熟練した
☐ experiment	実験
☐ experimental error	実験誤差
☐ expiration	（契約の）満了

☐	explanation	説明
☐	explicit	明確な
☐	explode	爆発する
☐	exploit	利用する
☐	exploration	調査
☐	exploratory drilling	試掘
☐	exposure	露出
☐	expropriation	没収
☐	extension cord	延長コード
☐	extent	範囲
☐	exterior	外面
☐	external	外部の
☐	extinct volcano	死火山
☐	extract	抽出する
☐	extraction	抽出
☐	extremely	極度に

F

☐	fabricated	組み立てられた
☐	facilitate	容易にする
☐	facility	設備
☐	facsimile	ファクシミリ
☐	factory	工場
☐	Fahrenheit	華氏
☐	failure	故障
☐	fat	脂肪
☐	fatigue	疲労
☐	fault	過失
☐	feasibility	可能性
☐	feasible	実行可能の
☐	feature	特徴

☐ ferroconcrete	鉄筋コンクリート
☐ fiber	繊維
☐ figure	図
☐ file	やすり
☐ fill orders	注文に応じる
☐ filter	濾過する
☐ filter paper	濾紙
☐ filtration	濾過
☐ fine	精巧な
☐ finished surface	仕上げ面
☐ finite	限定された
☐ fission	分裂
☐ fit	ぴったり合う
☐ fittings	備品
☐ fixation	固定
☐ flame	炎
☐ flammable material	可燃物
☐ flashlight	懐中電灯
☐ flask	フラスコ
☐ flat	パンクしている
☐ flaw	きず
☐ flexibility	柔軟性
☐ flexible	柔軟な
☐ floor plan	配置図
☐ fluid	液体
☐ fluorescent lamp	螢光灯
☐ flush	水洗いする
☐ foam	泡
☐ focal length	焦点距離
☐ focal point	焦点
☐ focus	焦点
☐ footnote	脚注

☐	force	（物理的な）力
☐	foreclose	除外する／防ぐ
☐	foregoing	前述の
☐	forging	鍛造
☐	formula	公式
☐	four-layer diode	4層ダイオード
☐	fraction	部分
☐	fragile	もろい
☐	fragment	破片
☐	framework	骨組
☐	free of charge	無料で
☐	freezing point	氷点
☐	frequency	周波数
☐	fresh water	真水
☐	friction	摩擦
☐	front-wheel-drive	前輪駆動
☐	frost	霜
☐	fuel	燃料
☐	fuel ash	燃料灰
☐	fuel gauge	燃料計
☐	fuel nozzle	燃料ノズル
☐	fuel-efficient	燃費効率の良い
☐	full line	実線
☐	full responsibility	全責任
☐	full-size	実物大の
☐	function	機能
☐	fundamentals	基礎
☐	furnace	炉
☐	furthermore	さらに
☐	fuse	ヒューズ
☐	fusible	可融性の
☐	fusion	融解

G

☐	gain	増加/利益
☐	galvanize	亜鉛めっきする
☐	gaseous	ガス状の
☐	gaseous fuel	気体燃料
☐	gasification	ガス化
☐	gage / gauge	計器/ゲージ
☐	galaxy	銀河（系）
☐	gallon	ガロン
☐	general-purpose	汎用の
☐	generate	発生する
☐	geometric	幾何学の
☐	geothermal	地熱の
☐	glass	ガラス
☐	glass fiber	ガラス繊維
☐	globe	球
☐	glove	手袋
☐	glow	白熱する
☐	grade	等級
☐	gradient	勾配
☐	grading	地ならし/整地
☐	gradually	徐々に
☐	grant of license	ライセンスの付与
☐	gravel	砂利
☐	gravitational	引力の
☐	gravity	重力
☐	grind	研磨する
☐	grinder	砥石
☐	groove	みぞ
☐	guarantee	保証する
☐	guess	推測する
☐	gunpowder	火薬

H

☐ hacksaw	弓鋸（ゆみのこ）
☐ harden	硬くする
☐ hardness	硬度
☐ hazardous	危険な
☐ head	先端部
☐ heat	熱
☐ heat shield	耐熱壁
☐ heat treatment	熱処理
☐ heat-treat	熱処理する
☐ height	高さ
☐ helical	螺旋状の
☐ hexagon	六角形
☐ high capacity machine	高性能な機械
☐ high mileage car	低燃費車
☐ high molecular	高分子の
☐ high technology	先端技術
☐ high-frequency	高周波
☐ homogeneous	均質な
☐ homogenize	均質化する
☐ horizon	地平線／水平線
☐ horizontal	水平の
☐ horsepower	馬力
☐ house	収容する
☐ humidity	湿度／湿気
☐ hydraulic	水力の
☐ hydraulic power	水力
☐ hydrocarbon	炭化水素
☐ hydrogen	水素
☐ hydrophilic	親水性の
☐ hydrophobic	疎水性の
☐ hyperbola	双曲線

☐ hypothesis　　　　　　仮説

I

☐ identify	確認する
☐ ignite	発火する
☐ ignition	点火（装置）
☐ illuminate	照射する
	／証明する
☐ imaginary	想像上の
☐ immediate	即座の
☐ immune	免がれた
☐ immunology	免疫学
☐ impair	悪くする
☐ impart	与える
☐ implement	実行する
☐ imply	暗示する
☐ impose	課する
☐ improper operation	誤操作
☐ impurity	不純物
☐ in connection with ～	～に関連する
☐ in series	直列に
☐ in the event of ～	～の時は
☐ in the interest of ～	～のために
☐ inactive	不活性の
☐ inadequate	不十分な
☐ incidence	発生状況
☐ inclined plane	斜面
☐ inclined to ～	～しやすい
☐ incoming	到来する
☐ incorporate	組み入れる
☐ incurred in ～	～に伴う

☐	indefinitely	無限に
☐	indemnify	補償する
☐	indemnity	損害賠償
☐	independent of ～	～と無関係で
☐	indicator	指示薬／指示器
☐	indispensable	不可欠な
☐	industrial complex	コンビナート
☐	industrial waste	産業廃棄物
☐	industry	産業
☐	ineffective	不良の
☐	inertia	慣性
☐	infer	推定する
☐	inferior	劣った
☐	inferior quality	粗悪な品質
☐	inflammable	可燃物
☐	inflation	膨脹
☐	information	情報
☐	informative	有益な
☐	infrared rays	赤外線
☐	ingredient	成分
☐	inhale	吸入する
☐	inherently	本来的に
☐	initial	初期の
☐	initial cost	原価
☐	initiate	始める
☐	injection	噴射
☐	injury	損傷
☐	inlet	入口
☐	innumerable	無数の
☐	inorganic	無機の
☐	inquiry	照会
☐	insignificant	重要でない

☐	insoluble	不溶性の
☐	inspection	検査
☐	inspection gauge	検査計
☐	install	据え付ける
☐	installation	取り付け
☐	instantaneous	瞬時の
☐	instruction	指示
☐	instrument	器具
☐	insufficient	不十分な
☐	insulation	絶縁
☐	insulator	絶縁物
☐	intake valve	吸気バルブ
☐	integrated circuit	集積回路
☐	intelligent quotient	知能指数
☐	intense	強烈な
☐	intensive	集中的な
☐	interaction	相互作用
☐	interchangeability	互換性
☐	interest	関心／利益
☐	interior	内部
☐	interlock	連動させる
☐	intermediate	中間の
☐	internal	内部の
☐	interpose	はさむ／挿入する
☐	interrupt	妨げる
☐	interstellar	(恒) 星間の
☐	interval	間隔
☐	introductory	入門の
☐	invalid	無効の
☐	invariable	不変の
☐	inventory	在庫
☐	inversely	正反対に

☐	invoice	請求書
☐	involved	関係する
☐	iodine	ヨウ素
☐	iron frame	鉄骨
☐	irradiate	照らす／発光する
☐	irregularity	不規則性
☐	irrespective of ～	～に関係なく
☐	irreversible	逆にできない
☐	isolate	分離する
☐	isolated	隔絶された
☐	isotope	同位元素
☐	item	項目／部品

J

☐	jack	ジャッキ
☐	jet	噴射
☐	junction	接合点
☐	joint	接続

K

☐	key	重要な
☐	kinetic energy	運動エネルギー
☐	klaxon	クラクション
☐	knob	つまみ／取手
☐	knot	結び目／要点

L

☐	labor arrangement	人員配置
☐	labor cost	人件費

☐	laboratory	実験室
☐	lack	不足（する）
☐	landmark	陸標
☐	lapse	時の経過
☐	laterally	側面方向に
☐	latest	最新の
☐	lathe	旋盤
☐	lattice	格子
☐	lava	溶岩
☐	layer	層
☐	lead	鉛
☐	lead-free gasoline	無鉛ガソリン
☐	leak	漏れ口
☐	leakage	漏れ
☐	length	長さ
☐	lengthen	長くする
☐	less than ～	～以下
☐	letter	文字
☐	liability	責任
☐	liable to	傾向にある
☐	liberated	遊離した
☐	licensed products	許諾製品
☐	lift pump	吸い上げポンプ
☐	lightproof	光を通さない
☐	linear	線形の
☐	liquefaction	液化
☐	liquefy	液化する
☐	liquid	液体
☐	liquid crystal	液晶
☐	liquid fuel	液体燃料
☐	liquid-cooling	水冷
☐	load	荷重

☐	location	位置
☐	loose	ゆるい
☐	loss	損失
☐	low-cost	安価な
☐	low speed	低速
☐	lower	降ろす
☐	lubricant	潤滑油／潤滑剤
☐	lubrication	潤滑
☐	luminosity	光度
☐	luminous	輝く

M

☐	machine tool	工作機械
☐	machined	機械加工の
☐	machinery	機械（装置）
☐	macroscopic	巨視的な
☐	magnetic device	磁気装置
☐	magnetic field	磁場
☐	magnetic tape	磁気テープ
☐	magnetism	磁力
☐	magnifying glass	拡大鏡
☐	maintain the quality	品質を維持する
☐	maintenance	保守／維持管理
☐	maintenance fee	維持費
☐	major premise	大前提
☐	majority	大多数／大部分
☐	malleable	可鍛性の
☐	malodor	悪臭
☐	man-day	延べ日数 ／マンデー
☐	man-made	人工の

☐ manifest	明らかな／明示する
☐ manipulate	手で扱う
☐ manual	マニュアル／取扱説明書
☐ manufacturer	製造メーカー
☐ manufacturing process	製造工程
☐ margin	余裕／マージン
☐ marine energy	海洋エネルギー
☐ mark	記号
☐ mass	**質量**
☐ mass production	大量生産
☐ material	材料
☐ materially	具体的に
☐ maximum	最大値
☐ mean	平均
☐ mean value	平均値
☐ measure	測定する
☐ measuring tape	巻き尺
☐ mechanics / dynamics	力学
☐ mechanism	メカニズム／仕組み
☐ medium	媒体／中間の
☐ melting point	融点
☐ merchandise	商品
☐ mercury	水銀
☐ mercury contamination	水銀汚染
☐ metal	金属／メタル
☐ metal stamping	金属加工
☐ meteor	流れ星
☐ meter	メートル
☐ methane	メタン

☐	metric system	メートル法
☐	microbe	微生物／病原菌
☐	microscope	顕微鏡
☐	microscopic	微視的な
☐	milling machine	フライス盤
☐	minimize	最小にする
☐	minimum	最小値／最小量
☐	minus	負
☐	mirror	鏡
☐	miscellaneous	種々の
☐	misleading	誤解させる
☐	missing	紛失した
☐	mixture	混合物
☐	modification	変更
☐	modulate	変調する
☐	modulation	変調
☐	moisture	湿度
☐	molecule	分子
☐	momentum	運動量
☐	mortar	モルタル
☐	mount	据え付ける
☐	mounting screw	取り付けねじ
☐	movement	運動
☐	multiplication	乗法
☐	multiply	掛け算をする
☐	mutual	相互の

N

☐	nail	釘
☐	namely	すなわち
☐	narrow	幅の狭い

☐	natural gas	天然ガス
☐	natural resources	天然資源
☐	negative	負の
☐	negative electrode	陰極
☐	neglect	無視する
☐	negligible	わずかな
		／無視できる
☐	negotiation	交渉
☐	neighboring	隣接の
☐	neutral	中立の
☐	neutralization	中和
☐	neutron	中性子
☐	nevertheless	それでもなお
		／やはり
☐	nitrogen	窒素
☐	noise	騒音
☐	non-conductor	不導体
☐	non-linear	非線形の
☐	nonetheless	それにもかかわ
		らず
☐	nonferrous metals	非鉄金属
☐	nonflammable	不燃性の
☐	normality	常態
☐	notch	刻み目
☐	notice	警告／注意
☐	noticeable	目立つ
☐	nuclear energy	核エネルギー
☐	nuclear reactor	原子炉
☐	nucleus	核
☐	numerical control	数値制御
☐	numerous	たくさんの
☐	nutrient	栄養分

○

☐	object	対象/目標
☐	obligation	義務
☐	oblique	傾いた
☐	observation	観察
☐	obtainable	手に入れやすい
☐	obtuse	鈍角の
☐	obviate	除去する
☐	obvious	明らかな
☐	occur	起こる/生ずる
☐	occurrence	発生
☐	octagon	八角形
☐	odd number	奇数
☐	odor	臭気
☐	ohm	オーム（単位）
☐	ohmmeter	オーム計
☐	oil	油（をさす）
☐	oil consumption	油消費
☐	oil filling	注油
☐	oil level	油面
☐	once	一度
☐	one dimension	一次元
☐	on-line	オンラインの
☐	opaque	不透明体（の）
☐	open	（回路を）開く
☐	opening	開口
☐	operate	操作する
☐	operating condition	使用条件
☐	operating cost	操業費
☐	operating procedure	操作手順
☐	operating temperature	運転温度
☐	opposite	反対の

☐	optical	光学の
☐	optimum	最適の
☐	optional	選択の
☐	orbit	軌道
☐	ordinance	条例
☐	ordinary	普通の
☐	ore	鉱石
☐	organic chemistry	有機化学
☐	orifice	（管の）口
		／開口部
☐	origin	起源
☐	oscillation	振動
☐	oscilloscope	オシロスコープ
☐	osmotic pressure	浸透圧
☐	outdistance	引き離す
☐	outermost	最外の／頂上の
☐	outlet	出口／コンセント
☐	outline drawing	概略図
☐	outset	最初
☐	outward	外向きの
☐	overall	全体の
☐	overestimate	過大評価する
☐	overhaul	分解検査
☐	overhead	一般管理費
☐	overwhelming	圧倒的な
☐	ownership	所有権
☐	oxidant	オキシダント
☐	oxidation	酸化
☐	oxide	酸化物
☐	oxygen	酸素
☐	oxygen cylinder	酸素ボンベ
☐	ozone layer	オゾン層

P

☐ packing	包装
☐ parabolic	放物線の
☐ parallel	平行／並列
☐ parallel lines	平行線
☐ part	部品
☐ particle	粒子
☐ particulars	詳細
☐ patch	あて物をする／パッチ
☐ patent	特許
☐ payment	支払い
☐ peel off	はがす
☐ pentagon	五角形
☐ per annum	１年につき
☐ performance	性能
☐ periodic inspection	定期検査
☐ peripheral	周辺の
☐ permanent	永久的な
☐ perpendicular	直角の／垂直の
☐ perpetual	長時間続く
☐ perpetual motion	永久運動
☐ personnel	要員／係員
☐ pertinent	関係のある
☐ petrochemical	石油化学
☐ petroleum	石油
☐ petroleum complex	石油コンビナート
☐ petroleum-short	石油不足の
☐ phase	局面
☐ phenomenon	現象
☐ photosynthesis	光合成
☐ physics	物理

☐ pickle	酸洗いする
☐ pigment	色素／顔料
☐ pillar	柱
☐ plain	わかりやすい
	／明白な
☐ plane	かんな（をかける）
☐ plane section	平面
☐ platform	台
☐ plating	めっき
☐ play	動き
	／あそび（がある）
☐ pliers	ペンチ
☐ plug in	差し込む
☐ plumb	オモリ
☐ plywood	ベニヤ板
☐ pointer	針
☐ polarity	極性
☐ pollutant	汚染物質
☐ pollute	汚染する
☐ pollution	汚染
☐ polyethylene	ポリエチレン
☐ polymerization	重合
☐ porcelain	陶器
☐ positive	積極的な
☐ possibility	可能性
☐ postal charges	郵便料金
☐ potassium	カリウム
☐ potential	可能性
☐ potential market	潜在市場
☐ potentially	潜在的に
☐ powder	粉（末）
☐ power	電力

☐	power conversion	電力変換
☐	power plug	電源プラグ
☐	power source	電源
☐	practicable	実行できる
☐	practically	実際は
☐	precaution	予防措置 ／注意事項
☐	precede	先に起こる
☐	precious metals	貴金属
☐	precipitation	沈澱
☐	precision	精密さ
☐	predetermined	あらかじめ決めた
☐	predominant	有力な／優勢の
☐	prefabricated house	プレハブ住宅
☐	prefer	好む
☐	preliminary test	予備試験
☐	preload	予圧
☐	preparation	準備
☐	pressing	プレス加工
☐	pressure	圧力
☐	presume	仮定する
☐	prevailing	優勢な
☐	prevention	妨害
☐	principal	主な
☐	principle	原理
☐	prior	事前の
☐	priority	優先順位
☐	probable	ありそうな ／有望な
☐	probe	調査
☐	procedure	手順
☐	proceed	続ける

☐	proceedings	記録集
☐	proceeds	売り上げ
☐	produce	生産する/生ずる
☐	product storage	製品貯蔵
☐	production	生産
☐	production cost	生産費
☐	profit	利益
☐	progressively	漸進的に
☐	prohibit	禁ずる
☐	project	投射
☐	project schedule	工程表
☐	projectile	発射体
☐	projection	投影/映写
☐	prolong	延長する
☐	promising	見込みのある
☐	promoter	促進剤
☐	prone to ~	~しやすい/傾向がある
☐	pronounced	はっきりした/著しい
☐	propellant	推進剤
☐	property	性質
☐	proportion	比例
☐	proportional	比例した
☐	protect	保護する
☐	protecting barrier	障壁
☐	protective coat	防護服
☐	protective coating	保護被覆
☐	protein	蛋白質
☐	prototype	原型/試作品
☐	protractor	分度器
☐	provide	供給する

☐ provided that ～	もし～ならば
☐ provision	準備／規定
☐ pulley	滑車
☐ pulse	脈
☐ purchase	購入
☐ purity	純度
☐ purpose	目的

Q

☐ quadratic equation	二次方程式
☐ qualifications	資格／適性
☐ qualitative analysis	定性分析
☐ quality	品質
☐ quality control	品質管理
☐ quality standards	品質規格
☐ quantitative	量的な
☐ quantitative analysis	定量分析
☐ quantity	量（数量）
☐ quenching	焼き入れ
☐ quotation	引用／見積もり

R

☐ radial	放射状の
☐ radiant heat	放射熱
☐ radiate	放射する
☐ radical	（数学／化学）根
☐ radio station	無線局
☐ radio wave	電波
☐ radioactive	放射性の
☐ radioactivity	放射能

☐ radius	半径
☐ random	無作為の
☐ rapid	急速な
☐ rapid cooling	急冷
☐ rate	割合
☐ rated	定格の
☐ ratio	比／比率
☐ raw material	原料
☐ ray	光線／熱線
☐ reaction	反応
☐ reagent	試薬
☐ rear	後部
☐ rearview mirror	バックミラー
☐ receiver	受信器
	／レシーバー
☐ receptacle	差し込み
☐ reciprocation	往復運動
☐ reckon	計算する
☐ reconditioning	再調節
☐ recovery	回収
☐ recovery process	回収工程
☐ rectangle	長方形
☐ rectification	整流
☐ rectify	整流する
☐ recycle	再生利用する
☐ reddish	赤みのかかった
☐ reduce	減ずる
☐ reduced scale	縮尺
☐ reduction	低減
☐ redundant	余計な
☐ reference	参照
☐ refine	精製する

☐ reflect	反射する
☐ reflector	反射板
☐ refraction	屈折
☐ refrigeration	冷却
☐ refund	払い戻す
☐ refuse	ごみ／廃物
☐ refuse dump	ごみ捨て場
☐ regardless of ～	～と無関係に
☐ region	領域
☐ registration fee	登録料
☐ regular maintenance	定期保守
☐ regularity	規則性
☐ regulate	調節する
☐ regulation	規定
☐ reinforced concrete	鉄筋コンクリート
☐ reinforcement	強化
☐ reject	除く
☐ relatively	相対的に
☐ release	放す
☐ reliability	信頼性
☐ remainder	残り
☐ remarkable	著しい
☐ removable	取り外せる
☐ removal	除去
☐ remove	取り外す ／取り除く
☐ repair	修理
☐ repel	拒否する ／防止する
☐ replace	交換する
☐ replacement	交換
☐ reproduce	再生する

☐	reproduction	複写
☐	reputation	評判
☐	require	要求する
☐	requisite	必須の
☐	researcher	研究者
☐	reservoir	貯水場／タンク
☐	residual	残留している
☐	residue	残留物
☐	resistance	抵抗
☐	resistivity	低抗率
☐	resonance	共振
☐	resources	資源
☐	respective	それぞれの
☐	respectively	それぞれ／別々に
☐	restricted	限定された
☐	resulting	結果として生ずる
☐	retracted	引っ込んだ
☐	reversal	反転
☐	revision	改訂
☐	revival	復活
☐	revolution	回転
☐	right angle	直角
☐	right to sunshine	日照権
☐	rigidity	剛性／硬直
☐	rocket-borne	ロケット搭載の
☐	rod	棒
☐	rotation	回転
☐	rotten	腐敗した
☐	royalty	技術料／使用料
☐	rubber	ゴム
☐	rudder	方向舵
☐	rule	規則

☐	rule out	除外する
☐	ruler	定規
☐	run	作動する／運動する
☐	rust	さび
☐	rusty	さびた

S

☐	safety	安全
☐	safety glasses	保護メガネ
☐	safety shoes	安全靴
☐	saline	生理用食塩水
☐	salinity	塩分
☐	satellite	（人工）衛星
☐	satisfactory	満足な／十分な
☐	saturation	飽和
☐	save	節約する
☐	saving	省力化／節約
☐	scaffold	足場
☐	scale	はかり／尺度
☐	scatter	散乱する
☐	schematic	図表（の）
☐	screw	ねじ
☐	screwdriver	ねじ回し／ドライバ
☐	seal	密封する
☐	section	断面図
☐	security	安全
☐	segment	片
☐	semiconductor	半導体
☐	separation	分離

☐	sequence	連続
☐	series circuit	直列回路
☐	set up	組み立てる
☐	settlement	解決／決着
☐	sewage	下水
☐	sewer	下水道
☐	shaft	軸
☐	shape	形／形づくる
☐	sharply	厳密に
☐	sheathe	被覆する
☐	shield	防護する
☐	shift	転換
☐	shipment	出荷
☐	shop	工場／作業場
☐	side view	側面図
☐	significance	意義
☐	signify	意味する
☐	silicon	ケイ素
☐	silver	銀
☐	similarity	類似性
☐	simplify	簡素化する
☐	simulate	模擬実験する
☐	simultaneously	同時に
☐	site	部位
☐	sizable	かなり大きい
☐	slab	平板
☐	slantingly	斜めに
☐	slide calipers	ノギス
☐	slide fastener	スライドファスナー
☐	slide rule	計算尺
☐	sodium	ナトリウム

☐	soft metal	軟金属
☐	solar battery	太陽電池
☐	solar system	太陽系
☐	solder point	はんだの継ぎ目
☐	soldering	はんだ付け
☐	soldering iron	はんだごて
☐	solid	固体
☐	solid line	実線
☐	solidify	凝固する
☐	solubility	溶解度
☐	solute	溶質
☐	solution	溶液
☐	solvent	溶剤／溶媒
☐	sound	音
☐	space	宇宙
☐	specific	明確な／特定の
☐	specific gravity	比重
☐	specific heat	比熱
☐	specifications	仕様（書）
☐	specify	指定する
☐	spectroscope	分光器
☐	spectrum	スペクトル
☐	sphere	球
☐	spherical	球形の／球状の
☐	spillway	放水路
☐	spiral	螺旋（形の）
☐	splinter	破片
☐	split	割れる
☐	spontaneously	自然に／自ら
☐	spring	ばね
☐	square	正方形
☐	square meter	平方メートル

☐	square number	平方数
☐	stability	安定性
☐	stainless steel	ステンレス
☐	standard	規格
☐	stapler	ホチキス
☐	static	静的な
☐	static electricity	静電気
☐	stationary	固定された
☐	stationery	文房具
☐	statistics	統計
☐	steel	鋼
☐	steerable	操縦型の
☐	steering wheel	(自動車の)ハンドル
☐	stereograph	立体図
☐	stipulate	規定する
☐	stir	かき混ぜる
☐	stockpile	資材
☐	stop valve	止め弁
☐	storage	倉庫
☐	storage device	記憶装置
☐	store	蓄積する
☐	straight line	直線
☐	strain	歪み／張り
☐	stranded wire	より線
☐	stratum	層／地層
☐	streamline	流線
☐	strength	強さ／濃さ
☐	stress	応力
☐	stretcher	担架
☐	strip	帯／鋼帯
☐	stroboscope	ストロボ

☐	structural	組織上の
☐	structure	構造／建造物
☐	strut	支柱
☐	sturdy	頑丈な
☐	subcontractor	下請業者
☐	subject matter	主題
☐	subject to ～	～を受けやすい
☐	sublimation	昇華／純化
☐	submit	提出する
☐	subsequent	続いて起こる
☐	subsequently	続いて
☐	substance	物質
☐	substantially	大幅に
☐	substitute	代用させる
		／代替品
☐	substratum	基盤
☐	subtract	減ずる
☐	succeeding	続く
☐	successive	連続する
☐	suction	吸引／吸い込み
☐	suffice	十分である
☐	sulfuric acid	硫酸
☐	summarize	要約する
☐	summation	合計
☐	superior	すぐれた
☐	superiority	優位
☐	supersonic aircraft	超音速機
☐	supervise	監督する
☐	supplement	追加／補足
☐	supply	供給（する）
☐	support	支える
☐	surface	表面

☐ surface treatment	表面処理
☐ surmise	推量する
☐ surplus	余剰
☐ surprising	驚くべき
☐ surprisingly	不意に
☐ surroundings	周囲／環境
☐ survey	測量
☐ susceptible	影響を受けやすい
☐ swell	膨張する
☐ switch	スイッチ
☐ symbol	記号
☐ symmetry	対称
☐ synchronous	同時的な
☐ synopsis	大要／摘要
☐ synthesis	合成
☐ synthetic fiber	合成繊維
☐ synthetic resin	合成樹脂
☐ syphon	サイフォン

T

☐ T-square	T定規
☐ table	表
☐ tamper with	いじくる
☐ tap water	水道水
☐ technical assistance	技術援助
☐ technical terms	専門用語
☐ technology	技術
☐ telescopic	伸縮自在の
☐ televise	テレビで放送する
☐ temperature	温度
☐ tempering	焼き戻し

☐	temporary	一時の
☐	ten thousand	1万
☐	tendency	傾向
☐	tender	入札する
☐	tenfold	10倍の／10倍に
☐	tensile	張力の
☐	tension	張力
☐	tentative	試験的な
☐	term of agreement	契約期間
☐	terminal	端子
☐	terms	条件
☐	terms and conditions	基本条件
☐	terrain	地域／地勢
☐	test tube	試験管
☐	tetrahedron	四面体
☐	theoretical	理論的な
☐	thermal conductivity	熱伝導度
☐	thermal efficiency	熱効率
☐	thermometer	温度計
☐	thermostat	サーモスタット
☐	thick line	太線
☐	thin	薄い
☐	thinner	シンナー
☐	third party	第三者
☐	thorough	完全な／徹底的な
☐	thread cutting	ねじ切り
☐	thrust	推力
☐	thyristor	サイリスタ
☐	tighten	しっかり締める
☐	tilt	傾ける
☐	tin	錫
☐	tin plate	ブリキ

☐ tissue	組織
☐ to the effect	その旨／～という趣意
☐ tolerable	耐えられる
☐ tolerance	許容（範囲）
☐ torque	トルク
☐ torsion	ねじれ
☐ total amount	総計
☐ total load	全荷重
☐ trace	痕跡
☐ track	軌道
☐ traction	牽引
☐ trade name	商号
☐ trademark	商標
☐ traffic density	交通量
☐ transfer	移転させる
☐ transformer	変圧器
☐ transmission	送信
☐ transmit	送信する
☐ transparent	透明な
☐ treatment	処理
☐ trial run	試運転
☐ triangle	三角形
☐ trifling	わずかな／役に立たない
☐ tripod	三脚台
☐ troubleshooting	故障発見
☐ troublesome	面倒な
☐ tune-up	調整
☐ tunnel	トンネル
☐ turbulent	乱流の
☐ tweezers	ピンセット

☐ twist	ねじれ／ねじる
☐ two-thirds	3分の2

U

☐ ultimate	究極の
☐ ultrasonic wave	超音波
☐ ultraviolet ray	紫外線
☐ unaffected	影響されない
☐ undercarriage	車台
☐ underestimate	過小評価する
☐ undesirable	好ましくない
☐ undoubtedly	疑いなく
☐ uniformly	一様に
☐ unit	単位
☐ universal	万能の
☐ universal joint	自在継手
☐ universe	宇宙
☐ unknown	未知の
☐ unplug	プラグを抜く
☐ unrecognized	未確認の
☐ unrelated	関連のない
☐ upgrade	質を高める
☐ uppermost	最上／最高の
☐ uranium	ウラニウム
☐ usable	使用できる
☐ utilization	利用
☐ utilize	利用する

V

☐ vaccine	ワクチン

☐ vacuum	真空
☐ vacuum cleaner	電気掃除機
☐ vacuum-tight	空気の入らない
☐ valence	原子価
☐ valid	有効な
☐ validity	妥当性
☐ value	数値
☐ vapor / vapour	蒸気
☐ variable	変数／可変の
☐ vehicle	車
☐ vein	静脈
☐ velocity	速度
☐ ventilator	換気装置
☐ verification	照合／立証
☐ verify	立証する／証明する
☐ versatile	多用途の
☐ vertical line	垂直線
☐ vessel	容器
☐ vibrate	振動する
☐ vibration	振動
☐ view	展開図
☐ vinyl	ビニール
☐ virtually	実質的には／事実上
☐ virus	ウイルス
☐ viscosity	粘度
☐ viscous	粘性の
☐ vise	万力
☐ visible ray	可視光線
☐ void of	欠けている
☐ volatile	揮発性の

☐	volatility	揮発性
☐	volcanic	火山の
☐	volt	ボルト
☐	voltage	電圧
☐	voltage detector	検電機
☐	voltage drop	電圧降下
☐	voltmeter	電圧計
☐	volume	容積

W

☐	wage regulations	賃金規定
☐	warehouse	倉庫
☐	warranty	保証（書）
☐	waste water treatment	排水処理
☐	waterproof	防水の
☐	watt	ワット
☐	wavelength	波長
☐	wax	ろう
☐	wear	摩耗
☐	wedge	くさび／ウェッジ
☐	weigh ～	重さが～である
☐	weight	重さ
☐	weld	溶接する
☐	welder	溶接工
☐	welding	溶接
☐	wetting agent	界面活性剤
☐	wheel	車輪
☐	width	幅
☐	windshield	フロントガラス
☐	wipe	拭き取る
☐	wiring	配線

☐ within 30 days	30日以内で
☐ withstand	耐える
☐ wood lathe	木工旋盤
☐ word processor	ワープロ
☐ workbench	作業台
☐ workmanship	技量
☐ workpiece	加工品
☐ workshop	仕事場
☐ worn	摩耗した
☐ wrist watch	腕時計
☐ written consent	書面の同意

X

☐ X-axis	X軸
☐ X-ray	X線

Y

☐ yard	広場／ヤード
☐ yarn	糸／ヤーン
☐ yearly	年間の
☐ yeast	酵母
☐ yield	生産高／生産する／許す

Z

☐ zinc	亜鉛
☐ zincate	亜鉛酸塩
☐ zonal	帯状の
☐ zone	地域
☐ zoology	動物学

「技術英検」実施団体の変更について
技術英語関連の全事業が一般社団法人日本能率協会（JMA）に移管されたことにより、「技術英検」の実施団体がJMAに変更になりました。
JMA内に設置されたJSTC技術英語委員会が事務局として「技術英検」の運営窓口となります。

技 術 英 語 ハンドブック

1987 年 3 月 30 日	第 1 版第 1 刷発行
1995 年 1 月 30 日	第 2 版第 1 刷発行
2020 年 3 月 30 日	改題第 1 刷発行
2022 年 12 月 15 日	第 5 刷発行

編著者——— 公益社団法人日本工業英語協会
©1978 JAPAN SOCIETY FOR TECHNICAL COMMUNICATION

発行者——— 張　士洛

発行所——— 日本能率協会マネジメントセンター

〒103-6009　東京都中央区日本橋 2-7-1　東京日本橋タワー
TEL　03(6362)4339（編集）／03(6362)4558（販売）
FAX　03(3272)8128（編集）／03(3272)8127（販売）
https://www.jmam.co.jp/

装丁——————— 冨澤　崇（EBranch）
印刷・製本所——— 広研印刷株式会社

ISBN978-4-8207-2788-0 C3282
落丁・乱丁はおとりかえします。
PRINTED IN JAPAN